Health and Safety Executive

Asbestos: The analysts' guide for sampling, analysis and clearance procedures

GW00500134

HSE Books

Contents

1 Introduction

What does this guidance do?

1.1   This publication consolidates and updates technical guidance from a number of HSE sources, including previously published guidance notes (EH10, MDHS39, MDHS77), which it now replaces. It mainly deals with analysts involved in licensed asbestos removal and sampling of asbestos-containing materials (ACMs). Simpler procedures are applicable for small scale and short-term asbestos removal work (*Asbestos essentials*)[1] and for ACMs which do not require a licence, eg asbestos cement (HSG189/2).[2] In addition, the publication links in with guidance produced for licensed removal contractors entitled *Asbestos: The licensed contractors' guide*.[3] This publication contains guidance on:

■   quality assurance;
■   training for analysts;
■   bulk sampling and analysis;
■   air sampling and analysis;
■   enclosures;
■   site certification for reoccupation;
■   supervisory work;
■   personal protective equipment; and
■   decontamination procedures.

1.2   Appendix 1 contains details of the future approved analytical method for the evaluation of fibres in air. Amendments to the European Worker Protection Directive[4] to be implemented by 2006 will replace the existing European Reference Method (see MDHS39/4)[5] with the World Health Organisation (WHO) method.[6] The updated method has been included to allow analysts to become familiar and train with the new method but MDHS39/4[5] should continue to be used until the new EU directive is implemented. Appendix 2 gives the analytical method for the identification of asbestos fibres in materials and contains the same advice as the last version of MDHS77.[7]

1.3   Although this guidance covers sampling and analysis of suspected ACMs, it does not go into detail about surveying and assessment of premises for ACMs. Surveying is covered in depth in MDHS100[8] and further guidance on the assessment and management of asbestos in buildings is given in HSG227.[9]

Who is this guidance for?

1.4   This guidance is designed for a technical audience, eg asbestos analysts, asbestos consultants, occupational hygienists, safety officers etc. It will also be useful to asbestos removal contractors and supervisors, employers, building owners and people with responsibility for managing properties and estates.

Legislation

1.5   The Control of Asbestos at Work Regulations 2002 (CAWR)[10] applies to all work activities involving asbestos-containing materials. It places duties on an employer, including the self-employed, who carries out, 'any work which exposes or is liable to expose any of his employees to asbestos…' to protect all employees and anyone else who may be affected by the work. There is also a specific duty under CAWR[10] to manage asbestos in buildings to ensure that asbestos is kept in good condition and to prevent uncontrolled work or releases.

1.6   CAWR[10] 2002 is supported by three Approved Codes of Practice that give practical guidance on how to comply with the law. Although failure to observe any of the provisions of an ACOP is not in itself an offence, that failure may be taken by a court in criminal proceedings as proof that a person has contravened the Regulations to which the provision relates. The onus would then be on that person to show that they have complied with the Regulations in an equally effective way. The three ACOPs are described in paragraphs 1.7-1.9.

1.7   *Work with asbestos which does not normally require a licence*,[11] applies to work on, or which disturbs, building materials containing asbestos; asbestos sampling; laboratory analysis and to the limited, permitted remaining work with asbestos during manufacturing.

1.8   *Work with asbestos insulation, asbestos coating and asbestos insulating board*[12] applies to work defined in the Asbestos (Licensing) Regulations 1983 (ASLIC),[13] for which a licence is required from the Health and Safety Executive (HSE). It also applies to employers carrying out similar work with asbestos insulation, asbestos coating and asbestos insulating board using their own employees on their own premises, who are exempted from the requirement to hold a licence under regulation 3(2) of ASLIC.[13]

1.9   *The management of asbestos in non-domestic premises*[14] provides advice on the duties under regulation 4 of CAWR[10] to manage the risk from asbestos in non-domestic premises. It explains the duties of building owners, tenants, and any other parties who have any legal responsibility for the premises. It also sets out what is required of people who have a duty to co-operate with the main duty holder to enable them to comply with the regulation.

1.10   Employers must consult safety representatives appointed by recognised trade unions under the Safety Representatives and Safety Committees Regulations 1977[15] with regard to health and safety issues. Employees not covered by such representatives must be consulted, either directly or indirectly, via elected representatives of employee safety, according to the Health and Safety (Consultation with Employees) Regulations 1996.[16]

1.11   Reference to legislation is made at appropriate points throughout this guidance.

Health effects

1.12   Asbestos-related diseases are currently responsible for more than 4000 deaths a year in the UK and the number is still increasing. Asbestos kills more people than any other single work-related illness. The diseases can take from 15-60 years to develop - so the person who has breathed in the fibres will not be immediately aware of any change in their health. There is an increased risk of ill health associated with exposure to amphibole asbestos fibres (eg amosite, crocidolite) in comparison with chrysotile (Hodgson and Darnton, 2000).[17]

1.13   Asbestos can cause two main types of disease in humans: cancer, particularly mesothelioma and lung cancer; and asbestosis (scarring of lung tissue). Other lung changes such as pleural plaques and diffuse pleural thickening, which are much less disabling, may be indicative of asbestos exposures, but can be due to other causes. New cases of asbestosis are now rare in the UK.

What is mesothelioma?

1.14   Mesothelioma is a cancer of the cells that make up the lining around the outside of the lungs and inside the ribs (pleura), or around the abdominal organs (peritoneum). By the time it is diagnosed, it is almost always fatal. Like other asbestos-related diseases, mesothelioma has a long latency period from first exposure to the onset of disease, on average 30-40 years.

What is lung cancer?

1.15   Lung cancer is a malignant tumour of the lungs' air passages. The tumour grows through surrounding tissue, invading and often obstructing air passages. The time between exposure to asbestos and the occurrence of lung cancer is on average 20-30 years. It should be noted that there is a synergistic effect between smoking and asbestos exposure which significantly increases the risk of developing lung cancer.

What is the risk to analysts?

1.16   All entry into enclosures carries a risk of exposure to airborne fibres. Analysts entering enclosures while removal or remediation work is being carried out will be potentially exposed to asbestos fibre concentrations above the control limits. Enclosure entry for other reasons such as bulk sampling or clearance inspections and air sampling will encounter lower airborne levels.[18] However, any direct disturbance of asbestos during these situations (eg brushing) can potentially give rise to short-term high exposure. It is important to be aware that as personal exposure is normally underestimated by static monitoring including clearance sampling, such results will not necessarily reflect personal exposure. Therefore regular personal monitoring should be carried out to assess individual risks and confirm the adequacy of respiratory protection. It is recommended that personal monitoring is performed in 10% of jobs involving enclosure entry.

Health surveillance

1.17   Under regulation 21 of CAWR 2002,[10] medical surveillance and health records are required for an employee if the exposure of that employee is likely to exceed the action level (see paragraphs 5.24 to 5.27). The employer should assess the risks of exposure of his employees to determine the requirement for medical examination.

1.18   Analysts should not normally enter live enclosures. However there will be occasions when entry is necessary or required (eg for supervision or checking when there are no or insufficient viewing panels). The results of personal airborne monitoring (see paragraph 1.16) should be used to assist in the risk assessment.

1.19   If an employer decides on the basis of his risk assessment that medical examinations are required, further information can be found in the ACOP *Work with asbestos insulation, asbestos coating and asbestos insulating board*[12] and *Asbestos: The licensed contractors' guide.*[3]

The role of the analyst in asbestos work

1.20   The analyst may be involved in asbestos work in a number of different ways. Most analysts carry out sampling and analysis of bulk and air samples. Some laboratories holding supervisory licences will employ analysts in a supervisory role in asbestos removal (see Chapter 7). More generally however, the analyst's role has been developing and growing in importance over the years. Most recently CAWR 2002[10] increased the involvement of the analyst in site clearance procedures. The analyst now has greater responsibility and opportunities for professional judgement. The analyst is responsible for completing site clearance certification for the work area, and for issuing a certificate of reoccupation. In addition, some clients may request greater participation in the asbestos removal work, including pre-clearance inspections and surveys, and site management and monitoring, eg overseeing the smoke test and carrying out some reassurance air sampling during the course of the contract.

1.21   Although not a legal requirement, it is desirable that the analyst is employed by the building owner or occupier for site clearance certification. This arrangement avoids any conflict of interest (perceived or real) that may arise should the analyst be employed by the removal contractor. It also enables an independent party to be involved in resolving any problems that arise during the clearance process. In addition, it has a practical advantage in that all results and certificates of reoccupation can also be issued directly to the person who has responsibility for the premises as well as to the contractor.

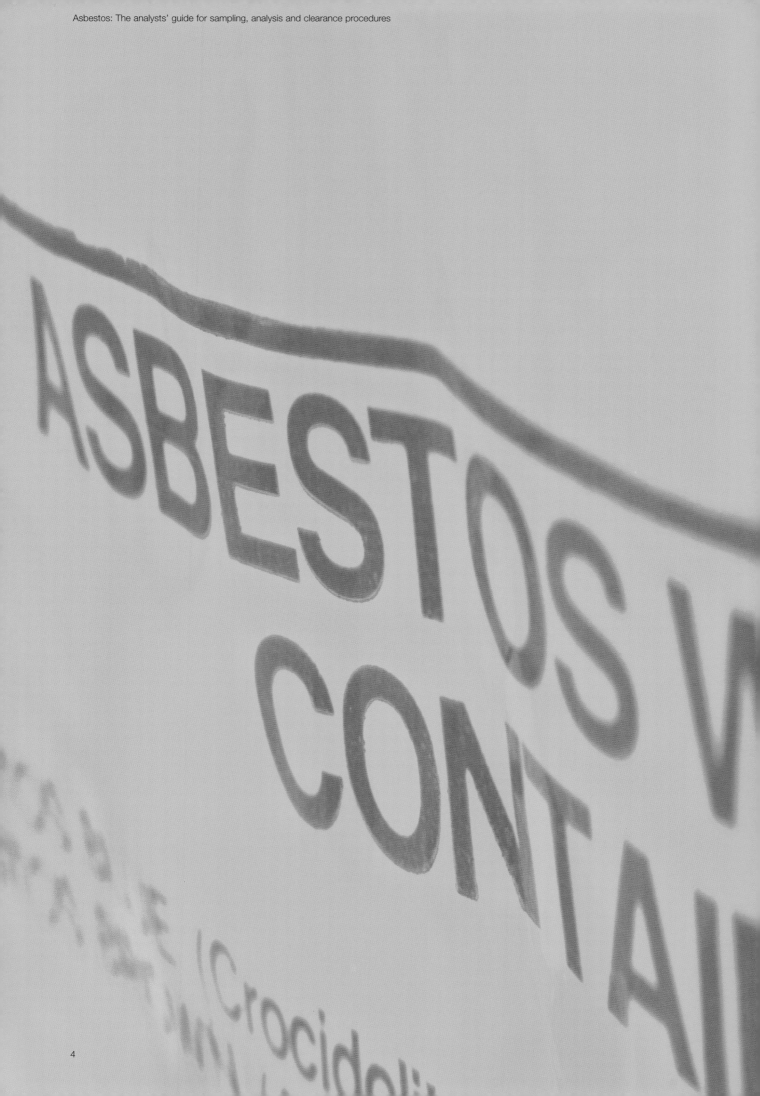

2 Quality assurance and accreditation schemes

2.1 Regulation 19 of CAWR 2002[10] requires that employers who use laboratories to undertake air sampling and analysis of air samples should assure themselves that the laboratory conforms with the competence standard ISO/IEC 17025.[19] Regulation 20 of CAWR 2002,[10] which came into effect on 21 November 2004, also requires that employers who engage laboratories to analyse asbestos materials assure themselves that the laboratory also conforms with ISO 17025. Conformation with ISO 17025 is demonstrated by obtaining accreditation from a recognised body. The United Kingdom Accreditation Service (UKAS) is currently the sole recognised accreditation body in Great Britain. The UKAS document which details the accreditation requirements and procedures (UKAS publication LAB 30 *Application of ISO/IEC 17025 for asbestos sampling and testing*)[20] is published on the internet, and can be downloaded from their website, www.ukas.com.

2.2 The asbestos site clearance certification process requires activities to be undertaken by accredited laboratories. The air sampling requirement is outlined in paragraph 2.1. The visual inspection procedures should be undertaken by laboratories that can demonstrate compliance with ISO 17020.[21] UKAS is also offering accreditation for this activity but ISO/IEC 17025[20] remains the lead standard. Separate UKAS accreditation for surveying buildings for ACMs under ISO 17020[21] is also available to laboratories. Individual accreditation under ISO/IEC 17024[22] will also be available in the near future. Accredited laboratories, and the specific methods the accreditation covers, are listed at www.ukas.org. Further information can be obtained from UKAS.

2.3 This document specifies additional requirements for laboratories that undertake air or material sampling. Those laboratories that analyse air samples must take part, and achieve a satisfactory standard, in an external quality assurance scheme for analysis of air samples. This requirement is set out in Appendix 1. The scheme is called the Regular Inter-laboratory Counting Exchange (RICE). It is administered by the Health and Safety Laboratory (HSL) on behalf of HSE and overseen by the Committee on Fibre Measurement (CFM).

2.4 The scheme for the identification of asbestos in materials is called the Asbestos in Materials Scheme (AIMS). This scheme is also administered by HSL on behalf of HSE and overseen by CFM. Participation and the maintenance of a satisfactory performance in this scheme is a requirement of Appendix 2 of this guidance. Further information and contact details on both schemes can be found on HSL's website at www.hsl.gov.uk.

3 Training and qualifications

3.1   Regulation 9 of CAWR 2002[10] requires employers to ensure that adequate information, instruction and training are given to their employees who are liable to be exposed to asbestos. The aim of this regulation is to ensure that employees are equipped with the relevant skills and knowledge to enable them to work safely by minimising their exposure to asbestos. Training alone does not make people competent. Training must be consolidated by practical experience so that the person becomes confident, skilful and knowledgeable in practice on the job. The ACOP, *Work with asbestos, which does not normally require a licence*,[11] paragraphs 52-56, sets out in some detail the areas of training that need to be covered when working with asbestos.

3.2   When drawing up a training programme for asbestos analytical staff, the training manager will first need to review the functions that the analyst will undertake. There will be different training needs for different functions. Functions will include:

- laboratory-based analysis of air and bulk samples;
- sampling surveys for asbestos in buildings;
- clearance of enclosures and hygiene facilities;
- supervisory licence work.

The training will normally consist of the following areas:

- organisation-specific training;
- health and safety training;
- function-specific training and qualifications;
- ongoing/refresher training and assessment.

Organisation-specific training

3.3   This may cover a range of topics associated with the established working procedures. It will usually include many items associated with ISO 17025 accreditation.

Health and safety training

3.4   The training manager needs to devise or source training programmes that include:

- the health effects of exposure to asbestos fibres;
- methods to reduce the risk when working with asbestos;
- safe handling and use of chemicals;
- ergonomic issues and requirements;
- company health and safety policy and procedures;
- selection, fitting, wearing and care of respiratory protective equipment (see Chapter 8);
- use of personal protective equipment;
- the meaning and interpretation of action and control levels and clearance indicator levels;
- emergency procedures.

Field staff training will also need to address topics such as:

- working in confined spaces;
- working at heights;
- lone working;
- working in hot environments;
- decontamination procedures.

Field staff who have to enter enclosures will have to complete practical training on RPE and decontamination as detailed in modules 24 and 25 of *Asbestos: The licensed contractors guide*[3] (see also Chapter 9).

Function-specific training and qualifications

3.5   Part of the accreditation process requires analytical laboratories to demonstrate that their employees are competent. Accreditation requires at least one senior member of an accredited laboratory's team to hold the British Occupational Hygiene Society (BOHS) Certificate of Competence in Asbestos. This BOHS Certificate is gained by two examinations, one written (S301 'Asbestos and other fibres') and one oral. BOHS can provide information regarding relevant courses and the written examination. It is not a requirement that a candidate sitting the S301 examination attends a training course. Once candidates have passed the written examination and have gained six months practical experience they can then apply to BOHS to sit the oral examination. A prerequisite of the oral examination is the submission of a written report on a suitable asbestos subject, often an asbestos survey, which must be acceptable to the examiners.

3.6   BOHS has also developed a series of five proficiency modules for training individuals in specific areas of asbestos work. These are:

- P401: identification of asbestos in bulk samples;
- P402: buildings surveys and bulk sampling for asbestos;
- P403: asbestos fibre counting;
- P404: air sampling and clearance testing of asbestos;
- P405: management of asbestos in buildings.

The accreditation process will require that all analysts carrying out asbestos work in the above areas must have, as a minimum, the appropriate P module or the S301 exam. This is being phased in and the P401 should currently be held by all analysts carrying out asbestos material analysis.

3.7   Each proficiency module is a stand-alone training course of 2-3 days duration, which is in a specific and individual area of asbestos work and covers both theory and practical training in the subject area. The aim of each proficiency module is to help individuals to become proficient to carry out the work covered by the module. All of the modules have practical assessments as well as a written examination. Any candidate who has been awarded a certificate of proficiency for all five modules will be deemed to have passed the written part of the S301 examination ('Asbestos and other fibres'). There would still be a requirement to pass the BOHS oral examination to be granted a certificate of competence. Details on training courses and course providers can be obtained from BOHS (see 'Further information' section).

3.8   Practical, on-the-job training is essential and should be carried out under the supervision of an experienced analyst to enable assessment of the trainee's competence. Accreditation requires that a laboratory has a documented training procedure which should include an element of supervised on-site experience. Internal and external quality control (QC) schemes are ideal for assessing competence (ie for the analysis of samples of airborne asbestos fibres and bulk analysis). Other procedures have to be developed in-house for air and bulk sampling – including site auditing before authorisation to carry out the task(s) unsupervised. Assessment of an analyst's competence must be confirmed by an appropriate senior laboratory member before any unsupervised site work.

3.9   Training for those fulfilling the function of a supervisory licence-holder (SLH) should cover all the subjects, at an appropriate level, in training modules 1-19 and 24-27 listed in Chapter 4 and Appendices 1 and 2 of *Asbestos: The licensed contractors' guide*.[3] Where relevant BOHS qualifications are held, a training needs analysis should be used to identify the outstanding modules that are required. It is anticipated that future BOHS courses will be modified to reflect these training modules and thereby reduce the training load.

Ongoing/refresher training

3.10   If an analyst is required to carry out more functions, additional training for those functions will be necessary. The ACOP L27[11] states that refresher training should be carried out on an annual basis for those whose work regularly disturbs asbestos. This refresher training should be relevant to the needs of the employee and to the work they undertake. For analysts this should include an update on any changes to guidance, ACOPs and regulations, a sharing and update of good practice and identification of bad practice, particularly in those areas of work that are difficult to measure, eg visual inspections, surveys.

3.11   The ongoing quality of the work carried out by analysts should be kept under review. For visual inspections related to providing certificates of reoccupation, other schemes need to be developed. A programme of accompanied/observed inspections on a regular basis would contribute to a successful internal quality assurance scheme. A briefing session or retraining might be the outcome of such an inspection. The importance of periodic and comprehensive internal auditing of analysts' performance cannot be over-emphasised.

4 Sampling and analysis of materials for the presence of asbestos

4.1   Sampling and analysis of materials for the presence of asbestos is normally undertaken to comply with CAWR 2002.[10] This may be as part of the duty to manage asbestos under regulation 4, or to comply with regulation 5. Regulation 5 requires employers of the people who are going to work with asbestos to identify the asbestos type(s) by analysis or to assume the material contains the most hazardous type(s) of asbestos (ie crocidolite and/or amosite). The purpose of the sampling is to collect representative samples of the suspect materials. The purpose of the analysis is to determine whether asbestos is present, and, if so, the type(s).

4.2   This chapter summarises the requirements for the sampling and analysis of suspected ACMs. Detailed information relating to the methods to be used in the analysis of materials for asbestos can be found in Appendix 2. MDHS100, *Surveying, sampling and assessment of asbestos-containing materials*[8] also covers sampling strategies and the reporting requirements for surveys in some depth.

4.3   Sampling ACMs can give rise to exposure to asbestos and is therefore also covered by CAWR 2002.[10] The Regulations require an assessment and plan of work to be made, and for the latter to set out the control measures and personal protective equipment (PPE) to be used. A generic risk assessment for sampling of ACMs should be supplemented by a site-specific risk assessment with appropriate control measures (see paragraph 4.4). It also requires that adequate information, training and refresher training have been given to the sampling personnel. Sampling ACMs is however, exempt from the Asbestos (Licensing) Regulations 1983[23] as amended.

Bulk sampling strategy

Safe systems of work

4.4   All sampling-related work must have an adequate risk assessment. The aim is to ensure that analysts and others including building occupants are not put at risk by the sampling. As well as the risks posed by the disturbance of asbestos, other hazards must be taken into account, in particular the risks from working at heights. It is recommended that surveys are conducted with two people working together. Two people are essential when work at height is involved and mandatory when dust control is employed, eg shadow vacuuming. Where working at heights is necessary, access platforms should be used where reasonably practicable to minimise the risk of a fall. Sampling personnel must wear adequate personal protective equipment, as determined by the risk assessment under CAWR.[10] The type of material sampled and the amount of disturbance of asbestos material will dictate the type of respirator. Airborne emissions should normally be controlled by pre-wetting the material to be sampled with water and/or a suitable wetting agent. Shadow vacuuming with a Type H vacuum cleaner should be used if wetting is likely to be incomplete or inappropriate (eg near live electrical equipment).

4.5   The areas to be sampled inside buildings should as far as possible be unoccupied and entry restricted during the sampling. The work should minimise the disruption to the clients' operations. The nature of the area and the likely release of dust will dictate the precautions required to prevent the spread of asbestos.

Strategy

4.6 Whether samples of suspect ACMs are being taken on an individual basis or as part of a survey, it is important that a sample(s) truly represents the location and the material from which it is taken. After assessing the extent of the material and any variations or repairs, representative samples of about 3-5 cm^2 area and through the entire depth of the suspect material should be taken. The samples must be representative of the whole material. Particular attention should be paid to ensure that the full inner edge or remote side are captured. Samples should normally be collected from the less conspicuous areas, or from where it causes least additional damage, eg the edges of tiles, boards and sheets or areas which have already been damaged.

4.7 The sampling strategy will be based on the types of ACM present. The following list is a guide to sample numbers and locations. However, a decision on the appropriate number of samples per location should be made after close inspection of the materials involved. More information is given on this in paragraphs 4.8-4.9.

- **Spray coatings, encapsulated sprays and bulk materials.** These are usually, but not always, homogeneous and normally two samples should be enough if taken at either end of the sprayed surface. More samples will be necessary if the installation is particularly large or there are areas of repairs or alterations.
- **Pipe/thermal insulation.** Pipe insulation is often highly variable in composition, especially where there is a change in colour, size and texture or where there is evidence of repairs or modifications. The number and location of samples will be dictated by the amount of variation and the planned or subsequent activities. Samples should initially be collected from areas that have no visible sign of having been patched or repaired. Areas to avoid include valves and hatches, or those close to access routes that are likely to be subject to repair and so less likely to contain asbestos.
- **Insulating board/tiles.** Insulating board is usually homogeneous but repairs may have been performed and/or replacement boards and tiles may have been fitted. One 3-5 cm^2 sample per room or every 25 m^2 is usually adequate. If there is evidently more than one type of panel then representative samples of each should be taken. When a material is visually consistent with asbestos insulating board, smaller samples may suffice as the amosite is readily detectable on analysis.
- **Asbestos cement materials.** These are homogeneous materials that are commonly encountered as corrugated and flat sheets or as various moulded products. In older buildings, most pre-formed exterior cement sheets are likely to contain asbestos so only limited sampling will be required to confirm the presence of asbestos. The risk from falls through asbestos cement roofs usually means that sampling is restricted. In some instances a strong presumption can be made that the material is asbestos, rather than trying to take a sample. One example of such a case is an asbestos cement flue. It is difficult to gain a sample without damaging the flue, which may lead to the release of harmful gases.

- **Other materials.** Where there are distinct types of materials, then one or two samples from each separate source will usually be adequate. Two samples are recommended if there are more than a few square metres of material. Examples of different materials include roofing felts and decorative coatings.
- **Debris and dust.** The sampling of debris can be carried out by picking out individual pieces or fragments, which are visually consistent with potential or known ACMs, or have visible fibres. If the damage is new, debris may still be present directly underneath the area. However, if damage was due to previous maintenance or removal activities, it may only be found in the less accessible areas, which are unlikely to have been cleaned (eg cable trays, on suspended ceiling tiles or tracks or on the back of shelves). When there is no visible debris or fibres, dust should be collected from areas where the asbestos may have accumulated.

Number of samples

4.8 The number of samples collected will depend on the extent and range of materials present and the extent of variation within the materials. Information on the types of materials involved, including those from changes due to repair or refurbishment may be available from architect plans or other sources. These should be consulted where possible. However in many cases the normal starting point will be a visual examination and assessment to check the extent and consistency of the material or product. Sample numbers should reflect the extent of variation (including materials types, colour/shade, texture, depth, coating). Decisions will have to be made on the basis of judgement and professional experience. The human eye (without colour blindness) can discriminate between many different hues, provided they are side by side. Fewer samples will be necessary where items are clearly identical and the lighting is adequate. Different materials are often different colours so samples of each will be needed to confirm the presence or absence of asbestos. Areas with visual signs of repair, replacement or patching will not be representative of the main material (they may be a more recent non-asbestos replacement material) and sampling will have to take this into account.

4.9 Other non-visual senses can also be used to discriminate between materials. Both asbestos insulating board and asbestos cement usually have characteristic sounds when knocked. While this cannot be used to positively identify the material or that asbestos is present, the sound emitted from knocking wall panels does give a strong indication of a change of composition and indicates when further samples should be taken. Similarly, the surface roughness and thermal conductivity (whether the material feels cold or warm when your hand is held against it) are also useful indicators of a change in material type. Wherever there is evidence of variation in material composition, samples of all sections should be taken.

Bulk sampling procedures

4.10   Surfaces onto which asbestos debris may fall should be protected with a sheet of impervious material such as polythene, to prevent the spread of contamination and for the ease of clean-up. As ACMs are defined as any material containing any asbestos, it is vitally important that any cross-contamination between samples is avoided by adopting careful procedures and ensuring that any sampling equipment is thoroughly cleaned before reuse. After sampling all samples must be individually sealed in their own uniquely labelled container, which is then sealed in its own second container or polythene bag. Further information on labelling, packaging and transportation of asbestos samples is given in paragraphs A2.62 to A2.69. The sample area should be left clean with no evidence of debris from the sampling operation and any sampling points sealed to prevent the release of fibres. A variety of methods are used to reseal the sampling point (eg tapes and fillers). The method used should be pre-agreed with the client and be appropriate, long-lasting and effective. Tapes may peel from loose, hot or damp surfaces. Water-based fillers may shrink and fall out as they dry. Foam sealants are often flammable and may breach fire regulations. In circumstances where sampling cannot be conducted or it will prejudice the sampling agency (eg the area is already contaminated with asbestos debris, so it is not reasonable to expect the sampling agency to leave the area clean, or the surface is badly damaged or of a type which is difficult to seal), the client should be informed.

Sample and site labelling

4.11   Whenever a sample is collected, its unique ID label should also be recorded in any associated documentation, so that the sample origin can be traced at a later date. The sampling position at the site may also be labelled with the same identifier. Visual records such as marked-up plans and/or photographic records showing the location and extent of the installation are also effective ways of recording the sampling position and the location of the ACMs, as well as the spread and condition of debris, if present.

Bulk sampling method

Spray coatings
4.12   If the coating is totally encapsulated, it can be pre-injected with liquid around the sampling area, then carefully cut with a sharp knife or scalpel to lift a small flap to obtain a sample. Damaged areas of encapsulated spray insulation can be accessed more easily, but should be avoided if the area shows signs of previous repair. If the spray coating is uncovered, both wetting and shadow vacuuming may be necessary to reduce airborne emissions. As sprays are usually homogeneous, a surface sample, which will cause little disturbance, should suffice.

Thermal/pipe insulation
4.13   Ideally, the area to be sampled should be fully wetted first; injection techniques are recommended. Precautions to avoid the spread of asbestos debris should be taken (eg a HEPA vacuum cleaner inlet or plastic bag held just below the area being sampled, with plastic sheeting on the floor beneath). Samples are taken with a core sampler, which

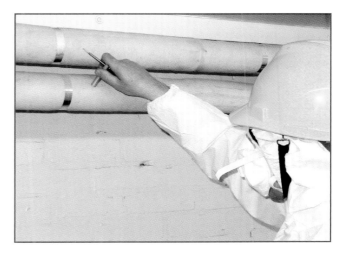

Figure 4.1 Analyst taking a core sample

should penetrate to the full depth of the pipe insulation (see Figure 4.1). Proprietary core samplers are available, which include caps or plugs to seal the ends of the tube. The core tube should be withdrawn through a 'wet wipe' and then sealed at both ends and placed in a labelled bag for transport back to the laboratory. Temporary plugs can also be made with 'wet wipes' by placing a wipe inside the tube before sampling and placing the external 'wet wipe' in the sampling end after it has been withdrawn. The sample point hole should be made safe after sampling (assuming that the pipe is to remain in place and the surface was originally intact). This helps to keep the insulation in good condition and to prevent the dispersal of asbestos. Where there is pipe insulation that is obviously new and non-asbestos, the possibility of debris from an earlier asbestos strip beneath the new insulation should be investigated.

Insulating board
4.14   Materials such as ceiling tiles or wall panels should be inspected for areas of existing damage as a sample can be collected more easily in these situations. Otherwise a small sample should be taken from a discreet location at the corner or edge of the panel, with a sharp knife or chisel blade to lever off a sample. The area to be sampled (if remote from any live electrical sources) should be wetted before sampling using a hand spray with a suitable wetting agent. Insulating boards may occasionally have been manufactured with asbestos paper on one or both sides.

Asbestos cement
4.15   Asbestos cement is usually very hard and it is preferable to seek a damaged portion where it will be easier to remove a small sample. The sample size should be at least 5 cm^2 as it will be necessary to search for traces of amphibole asbestos, such as crocidolite. The sample should be obtained using blunt-nosed pliers or a screwdriver blade to remove a small section from an edge or corner. **(Samples should not be collected from roofs without special safety precautions to prevent falls through the fragile sheets)**.

Gaskets, rope, seals, paper, felt and textiles
4.16   The material should be wetted. Samples can be taken using a sharp knife to cut a representative portion from the material.

Floor and wall coverings

4.17   Samples should be cut out with a sharp knife, usually taking one sample from tiles of each type or colour present. The fibre release is likely to be very low, unless the asbestos is present as a lining or backing material.

Textured coatings

4.18   Samples should be obtained by carefully prising off flakes of the coating and/or backing material, using a scraper. If applied directly to a resilient surface such as concrete, the removal of flakes will be difficult and it may be necessary to scrape the coating with a sharp chisel, to direct the material into a sample container held below the sampling point. As asbestos may not be uniformly present in the coating and the coating is usually thin, an area of about 20 cm^2 should be sampled. Note: You should check what the coating has been applied to – it could be AIB.

Debris and dust samples

4.19   Small fragments of debris released due to damage to ACMs or poor cleaning after removal of ACMs, can be picked up with a smooth pair of tweezers and placed directly into a sealable container or plastic bag. Dust samples can be collected in a number of ways: for example by turning a sealable plastic bag inside out and wiping it along the surface, before reversing and sealing the dust collected inside; by scraping the dust layer into a pile and transferring into a container; by sampling onto adhesive tapes and damp filter papers (note however that once the asbestos fibres are attached to the collection media, identification of the types of asbestos present is often not possible, as the fibres cannot be placed in the refractive index (RI) oil of choice and the RI of the collection media will interfere with the dispersion staining colours).

Sample analysis and reporting

4.20   The method used to examine the samples and to identify the type of asbestos present is given in Appendix 2. For many ACMs where the fibres are easy to find and pick out it involves four stages:

■   examination at X 10-X 40 in a stereo microscope for fibres and fibre bundles;

■   picking out of examples of the various fibre types seen and mounting in a RI liquid between a glass microscope slide and cover slip;

■   examination of the optical properties using polarised light microscopy (PLM) and dispersion staining techniques at magnification of X 100 or greater;

■   identification of the asbestos type present based on the observed optical properties (see Figure 4.2).

4.21   When the fibres are encapsulated in a matrix or covered with other fine particles, sample preparation is required to extract, concentrate and clean the fibres so that the optical properties can be viewed without interference. When no fibres are seen during the stereo-microscopy examination, the presence of fine fibres must be checked by examining small random samples at higher magnifications (X 100 or greater) using PLM or other microscopy techniques which will enhance the contrast or visibility of fine asbestos fibres.

Figure 4.2 An analyst carrying out asbestos analysis

4.22   All test reports must meet the requirements of ISO 17025[19] and must state clearly whether or not asbestos was found and give the types of asbestos identified. From 21 November 2004, laboratories have to have had UKAS accreditation for the identification of asbestos by PLM. To demonstrate continued competence in asbestos identification, the laboratory will also need to participate in the AIMS and maintain a satisfactory AIMS score (see paragraphs 2.1-2.4).

4.23   Although the method in Appendix 2 does not quantify the amount of asbestos present, it is recommended that 'asbestos not detected' is reported when no asbestos fibre is found after careful searching of the sample under the stereo microscope for 10 minutes and searching a minimum of two preparations mounted in suitable RI liquid at high magnification by PLM/PCM for a further 5 minutes. If during the search only 1 or 2 fibres are seen and identified as asbestos, the term 'trace asbestos identified' should be used. If there are fibres present which are too thin to be identified, the result should report that fine fibres were present, 'but too thin to identify'. If it is possible to give an opinion that the thin fibres appeared 'asbestos-like' or 'not-asbestos-like' this is permitted, as opinions do not constitute part of the UKAS-accredited analysis. The analytical method is not quantitative and percentages of asbestos should not be reported, however guidance on the percentage of asbestos used in various products is available in MDHS100.[8]

5 Sampling and analysis of airborne fibre concentrations

5.1   The CAWR 2002 ACOPs L27[11] and L28[12] give guidance on when monitoring of the airborne fibre concentration is appropriate and how records should be kept. Details are given in paragraphs 126-137 (L27)[11] and 179-185 (L28).[12]

5.2   Air sampling involves drawing a known flow rate of air through a filter for a measured time, so that airborne particles are collected. The filter is then prepared for microscopical examination. A known fraction of the filtered deposit is examined using X 500 phase contrast microscopy to count all fibres seen (particles >5 μm long, <3 μm wide and a length to width (aspect ratio) of >3:1) in a known number of graticule areas. The calculated total number of fibres collected on the filter is divided by the volume of air sampled to determine the fibre concentration in terms of fibre per millilitre of air (f/ml).

5.3   Personal sampling to comply with CAWR[10] and the ACOPs is used:

- to check the effectiveness of control measures, ie that engineering controls are working as they should, to their design specification and do not need maintenance or repair;
- to find out whether a control limit is exceeded so that appropriate RPE can be selected;
- to confirm that the RPE in use is capable of providing the appropriate degree of protection;
- to determine whether the action level is likely to be exceeded;
- for medical surveillance records;
- to support current and future risk assessments.

5.4   The fibre levels obtained in personal sampling will reflect the nature of the work performed by the operator and the circumstances and conditions at the time of sampling. Therefore it is essential that the analyst collects accurate information on the tasks performed by the worker during sampling (including duration) and on the other factors which will influence exposure including how the tasks were performed (tools, equipment etc and methods and techniques) and the controls that were employed. This information should be used to allow meaningful interpretation of the sampling results.

5.5   Static sampling to comply with CAWR[10] and the ACOPs is appropriate for:

- background sampling to establish fibre concentrations before any activity which may lead to airborne asbestos contamination;
- leakage testing to ensure that the steps taken to prevent the enclosure leaking are and remain effective and it is not releasing airborne respirable fibres;
- site certification for reoccupation on completion of asbestos removal work;
- reassurance sampling, which may be conducted in certain circumstances to confirm that the residual asbestos fibre concentrations are <0.01 f/ml. For example, after the removal of an enclosure; and
- static sampling to assess asbestos fibre concentrations inside enclosures before entry for a visual inspection.

5.6   Where employees are under medical surveillance, ie where an action level is exceeded, a summary of any air monitoring results available to the employer should be included in their health record. The employer must retain these records for 40 years from the last entry. Any monitoring results should be made available to the people sampled.

When monitoring is not necessary

5.7   Some typical situations when monitoring may not be required are:

- where there are good reasons for expecting that the exposures will be very low and well below the relevant control limit;
- during the four-stage clearance procedures where the removal work has been performed externally, eg soffit removal;
- where the work is a single event of such short duration/low emission that suitable monitoring results could not be obtained in the sampling time (ie the detection limit is more than the control limit);
- where adequate information is already available to enable the appropriate protective equipment to be provided; and
- where the protective equipment provided is of such a high standard relative to the known exposure for the work performed that no foreseeable measurement result could indicate a need for equipment of a higher standard.

The measurement method

5.8   The method of measuring airborne asbestos fibre levels is set out in legislation. CAWR 2002[10] requires that all air sampling measurements used to check compliance with an action level or control limit are obtained by an HSC-approved method. The current approved method is set out in MDHS39/4.[5] The method in Appendix 1 will replace the current approved method when the new European Worker Protection Directive[4] is enacted in the UK. This is likely to be in 2006. At this time MDHS39/4[5] will be withdrawn and replaced by Appendix 1.

5.9   The HSC-approved method must be strictly followed when sampling to check against the 4-hour control limit. However, sampling flexibility is allowed when comparison is to be made with the 10-minute control limits and the action levels. The sample flow rates can be varied to ensure that the density of the collected dust deposit is suitable for counting and that an adequate limit of quantification and precision is obtained. Further modifications in the approved method are permissible in other sampling situations. When airborne sampling results are needed very quickly (eg in enclosure checking and clearance certification), the method can be adapted to allow wider variations in flow rate, increased numbers of graticule areas to be counted and to allow discrimination between fibre types using other microscopy techniques. See Table 5.1 for a summary of the situation.

5.10   The method can interpret airborne fibre concentrations from the quantification limit (0.01 f/ml) up to a concentration of 100 f/ml. The sampling strategy should aim to achieve the optimum fibre density on the filter of 100-650 f/mm^2 of the filter area. The upper density limit of the range may be extended to 1000 f/mm^2 if few interfering particles are present, but may need to be reduced where many non-fibrous particles or agglomerates are present. However, at these higher levels there is increased undercounting by the analyst and results will underestimate the concentration.

5.11   The analytical sensitivity based on one half fibre counted in 200 graticules for a sample volume of air equivalent to at least 480 litres passed through a filter with an effective diameter greater than 20 mm is between 0.0002-0.0003 f/ml. However, due to background count levels on filters the limit of detection is about 0.003 f/ml and the limit of quantification of the method is set at 0.010 f/ml, equivalent to a count of 40 fibre ends (20 fibres) in 200 graticules (see A1.7-A1.8). If fewer than 20 fibres are counted, the calculated result will have an increased imprecision and it is normal to calculate and report the results as less than the limit of quantification (ie 20 fibres). In some circumstances it may be useful to calculate the actual result even if <20 fibres (40 fibre ends) are counted but any interpretation will have to take into account the level of precision of the counts on the actual filters and the associated blanks. The accuracy and precision of fibre counting are discussed further in paragraphs A1.42–A1.45 in Appendix 1.

Sampling strategies

5.12   MDHS39/4[5] and Appendix 1 of this guidance give details of the sampling technique and equipment to be used to collect samples for analysis. Paragraphs 5.13-5.22 outline the strategies to adopt when collecting samples.

5.13   Table 5.2 sets out the recommended sample flow rates and volumes and the number of graticule areas to be examined when carrying out air tests, depending on the purpose of air sampling. For samples with large numbers of fibres, stopping rules allow counts to be terminated after 100 fibres (200 ends) have been counted, provided at least 20 graticule areas have been assessed. In situations where a lot of non-asbestos dust is being generated, sample air volumes will need to be reduced to obtain countable samples. A series of sequential samples taken for shorter times and/or lower flow rates may be the only way to collect countable samples. The use and need for these and any other strategies adopted will need to be highlighted in the report, and the likely effects and biases on the results discussed.

Personal sampling for compliance under CAWR 2002[10] and to assess respiratory protection

5.14   The filter holder should point downwards and be fixed to the upper lapel or shoulder of the worker's clothing, as close to the mouth and nose as practicable, and preferably within 200 mm. Give due regard to localised concentrations: in such cases, the sampling head should be positioned on the side expected to give the higher result. If a respirator is worn, the sampling head should be positioned away from the clean air exhaust.

Background or reassurance sampling

5.15   During background or reassurance sampling, the distribution of measurement points should cover likely sources of fibre and likely areas of frequent human occupation. To achieve the quantification limit (0.01 f/ml), each measurement must result from a total of at least

Table 5.1 Summary of HSC approved methods

4-hour control limit	10-minute control limit	Action level	Enclosure checking and sampling for certification of reoccupation
HSC-approved method (MDHS39/4)[5]	HSC-approved method but with the sample flow rates varied		As detailed in Annex 1 of MDHS39/4[5]

Table 5.2 Recommended flow rates, minimum volumes and graticule areas examined versus the limit of quantification

Application	Sampling rate (litres/minute)	Minimum volume of air to be sampled onto 25 mm diameter filter (litres)	Minimum number of graticule areas to be examined	Airborne concentration at the limit of quantification (20 fibres counted) (fibres/millilitre)
Personal sampling				
4-hour control limit*	1	240	100	0.04
10-minute control limit	4	40	100	0.24
Action level (individual samples)	1-4	480	100	0.02
Assessment of respiratory protection	>0.2-4	40	100	0.24
Static sampling				
Clearance indicator	1-16	480	200	0.01
Background	1-16	480	200	0.01
Leak	1-16	480	200	0.01
Reassurance	1-16	480	200	0.01

* HSC-approved method specifies these values

480 litres in volume. Fewer measurements may be generated during background and reassurance sampling than for sampling for certification of reoccupation.

Leak testing

5.16   Measurement of the airborne fibre concentration outside the enclosure is used to determine whether the integrity of the enclosure is being maintained. Leak testing is used to support the initial smoke test and the frequent thorough visual inspections of an enclosure during removal work. A number of sample positions should be considered: for example, near the enclosure openings (eg near the three stage airlock, where the removal operatives enter and leave the enclosure and the baglock for

where the double bagged asbestos waste leaves the enclosure), near areas where there had been difficulty sealing the enclosure (eg pipe or cable penetrations) and near the exhausts of the air extraction system. For this type of testing it may be desirable to sample at higher flow rates. Paired sampling can also be used to shorten the sampling time required to achieve 480 litre samples. The cause of any fibres above background should be investigated.

Sampling for site reoccupation certification

5.17   Sampling for certification of reoccupation should take place only when the enclosure is dry and a visual inspection confirms that it is free from debris and dust. Practical advice on the preparation of the enclosure and the application of assessment for site reoccupation certification is given in HSG247[3] for licensed contractors and Chapter 6 of this guidance. Sampling equipment should be distributed throughout the enclosure with at least half the samplers close to or underneath where the asbestos was removed. The sampling heads should be located at a height between 1-2 m from the floor and filter holders should point downwards. In tall enclosures (eg vertical pipe work or lift shafts), samplers should be placed at representative exposure heights, especially in areas where residual dust may be difficult to detect. There should always be at least two measurements (unless the volume of the enclosure is less than 10 m², in which case one measurement is adequate). With that overriding condition, the number of samples should be at least the integer (whole number) next below ($A^{1/3}$–1) where A is determined as follows:

- if the enclosure is less than or equal to 3 m in height, or in enclosures which are higher than 3 m but where exposure is likely to be at ground level only, A is the area of the enclosure in square metres;
- in other cases, A is one third of the enclosure volume in cubic metres; if there are large items of plant (such as boilers) in the enclosure, their volumes may be subtracted from the enclosure volume before calculating A.

5.18   This formula has no theoretical significance, and merely serves to generate reasonable numbers. It gives the minimum appropriate number of measurements; however, personnel responsible for sampling may judge that more measurements than indicated by this minimum are required. Thus, a larger number of measurements than this minimum may be needed where an enclosure is obviously sub-divided, as for example when a whole floor of a building is comprised of many smaller rooms within the enclosure. Table 5.3 gives examples of the numbers of measurements required.

Table 5.3 Examples of the minimum number of measurements given by the formula ($A^{1/3}$–1)

Enclosure size		Number of measurements
Area (m²)	Volume (m³)	
N/A	<10	1
<50	150	2
100	300	3
200	600	4
500	1500	6
1000	3000	9
5000	15 000	16
10 000	30 000	20

5.19   Each measurement should be based on a sample volume of at least 480 litres. It is permissible to achieve a measurement by pooling two or more simultaneous or consecutive samples having a total of at least 480 litres. Samples that are pooled in this way should be taken within 1 m of each other and are regarded as a single measurement.

5.20   The purpose of the disturbance activity is to ensure that workers, occupants, cleaners and members of the public using the area in the future are not exposed to asbestos as a result of ineffective removal and cleaning. A realistic simulation of a possible future activity that may produce high airborne dust and fibre concentrations is the brushing or sweeping of surfaces. Brushing should be carried out in a manner that is consistent with normal cleaning activities in a building. Brushing should take place in all of the following locations: all surfaces from where the asbestos has been removed, horizontal surfaces where the dust may have settled or collected or where there is suspicion of surface contamination, and surfaces in close proximity to the sampling equipment. These dust-raising activities should be substantial enough to raise fine settled dust (if it is present) from surfaces, and should be commensurate with the size of the enclosure. They should take place for a duration of at least 1.5 minutes for each measurement point inside the enclosure, near the start of each full hour of sampling, or each time a new filter is used in an area. For larger enclosures there is likely to be more than one person carrying out the dust disturbance work, so the same total surface area will be disturbed but in less time. This means the total time of the disturbance is unlikely to exceed around 10-15 minutes each hour.

5.21   All brushes used for raising dust should be considered as being contaminated and should generally be disposed of as asbestos waste. However some brushes may have detachable screw handles. Where the handle is constructed from a material which could be effectively decontaminated (eg plastic) then this part may be reused after thorough cleaning. Brush heads, irrespective of the composition, should always be disposed of as asbestos waste.

Control limits, action levels and the clearance indicator for site reoccupation

Control limits

5.22   Control limits are concentrations of asbestos fibres in air averaged over any continuous 4-hour period or any continuous 10-minute period. Each time-related limit is a control limit in its own right. Worker exposure to asbestos fibres should be reduced to as low as is reasonably practicable and in any case below the control limits. Suitable RPE must be worn where exposure has the potential to exceed either of the limits.

5.23   In addition, for each of the time-based control limits, there are also two sets of numerical limits. The set to be used depends on the type of asbestos present during the work concerned. One set applies to chrysotile alone and the other set applies to all the amphibole forms of asbestos (ie crocidolite, amosite, asbestos actinolite, asbestos anthophyllite, asbestos tremolite and any mixture containing any of those minerals). The numerical limits are as follows:

- for chrysotile alone:
  - 0.3 fibres per millilitre of air, averaged over any continuous period of 4 hours;
  - 0.9 fibres per millilitre of air, averaged over any continuous period of 10 minutes;
- for any other form of asbestos, either alone or in mixtures, including mixtures of chrysotile with any other form of asbestos:
  - 0.2 fibres per millilitre of air, averaged over any continuous period of 4 hours;
  - 0.6 fibres per millilitre of air, averaged over any continuous period of 10 minutes.

5.24   Where the composition of asbestos material is not known, employers may choose to assume that the asbestos is not chrysotile alone and apply the more stringent limits; the type of asbestos need not then be identified. However, if a mixture of chrysotile and one or more forms of amphibole asbestos is present, the asbestos is not chrysotile alone, and the more stringent control limits must be used.

Action levels

5.25   Action levels apply to exposure in the longer term, and are cumulative exposures calculated over any continuous 12-week period. The 12-week period should not be chosen in such a way as to avoid exceeding an action level; it should represent a 'worst case' for the work undertaken. To calculate cumulative exposure, multiply each airborne respirable asbestos concentration by the time for which it lasts, and add up all these products over the 12-week period in question. The result is expressed as a number of fibre-hours per millilitre of air (fibre-hours per ml). Examples of how to calculate action levels are set out in Box 5.1.

5.26   Airborne respirable fibre concentrations can be estimated using available data or past experience of the process in question, but in cases of doubt it may be necessary to confirm the estimates by measurement using a method approved by HSC (see paragraphs 5.8-5.9). If the exposure of any employee exceeds or is likely to exceed an action level, the regulations 6, 8, 17 and 21 in CAWR 2002[10] on assessment, notification, designated areas and medical surveillance apply. The exposure of employees who regularly work with asbestos insulation and/or coatings for a contractor licensed by HSE under the ASLIC Regulations 1983 (as amended) will normally exceed an action level.

5.27   The action levels are:

- 72 fibre-hours per millilitre of air, where the exposure is solely to chrysotile; or
- 48 fibre-hours per millilitre of air, where exposure is to any other form of asbestos, either alone or in mixtures, including mixtures of chrysotile with any other form of asbestos.

Box 5.1 Examples of action level calculations

Example 1

An employee is exposed to a uniform airborne respirable asbestos concentration of 0.3 fibres/ml for 3 hours every working day. Over 12 weeks the cumulative exposure is:

$$0.3 \times 3 \text{ (hours)} \times 5 \text{ (days)} \times 12 \text{ (weeks)} = 54 \text{ fibre-hours/ml}$$

which is below the action level for chrysotile, but above that for all other forms of asbestos, including mixture.

Example 2

An employee is exposed to chrysotile at a concentration of 2 fibres/ml for a continuous 2-hour period each week for 10 weeks. In each of the next 2 weeks there are additional single exposures of 10 hours each at 1 fibre/ml. The total cumulative exposure is:

$$(2 \times 2 \text{(hours)} \times 10 \text{(weeks)}) + (1 \times 10 \text{ (hours)} \times 2 \text{(weeks)}) = 60 \text{ fibre hours/ml}$$

which is below the action level for chrysotile. This example shows how the control limit may be exceeded but not the action level.

Example 3

Employees stripping crocidolite insulation using a proprietary wetting agent/dust suppressant are exposed to an airborne respirable fibre concentration of 2 fibres/ml. The action level would be exceeded after 24 hours:

$$2 \times 24 \text{ (hours)} = 48 \text{ fibre-hours/ml}$$

Example 4

An employee is exposed to chrysotile at a concentration of 3 f/ml for 15 hours and at separately identifiable times to a concentration of 2 f/ml to an amphibole form of asbestos for 6 hours. In this example, one type of exposure can be clearly distinguished from the other. Applying the formula described in Box 5.2 to test if the combined action level is exceeded for mixed exposures:

$$\frac{\text{Exposure 1}}{\text{AL 1}} + \frac{\text{Exposure 2}}{\text{AL 2}} = \frac{15 \times 3}{72} + \frac{6 \times 2}{48} = 0.875$$

Which is less than 1, so the combined action level is not exceeded.

Box 5.2 Formula for calculating whether a composite action level has been exceeded

$$\frac{\text{Exposure 1}}{\text{AL 1}} + \frac{\text{Exposure 2}}{\text{AL 2}} \text{ is greater than } 1$$

Where:
Exposure 1 = the cumulative exposure to chrysotile;
Exposure 2 = the cumulative exposure to all other forms of asbestos either alone or in mixtures, including mixtures containing chrysotile;

and:
AL 1 = the action level for chrysotile;
AL 2 = the action level for all other forms of asbestos whether alone or in mixtures, including mixtures containing chrysotile.

Box 5.3 Example of a calculation of clearance samples for comparison with a clearance indicator

Enclosure is more than 4 m high. Volume 7500 m^3.
Enter A = 7500/3 = 2500, in (A$^{1/3}$–1). (A$^{1/3}$–1 is) = 12.6.
Twelve measurements are required.
Results obtained are: 0.008, 0.008, 0.004, 0.014, 0.003, 0.010, 0.002, 0.009, 0.008, 0.007, 0.004, 0.003 fibres/ml. At least 80% of these results are less than 0.010 f/ml, and all are less than 0.015 f/ml, so under the terms of paragraph 85 the air in this enclosure is acceptably clean.

5.28   If both types of exposure occur at separately identifiable times during the 12-week period concerned, a proportionate number of fibre-hours may be applied to a composite action level. Box 5.2 gives a formula to be used to decide whether or not the composite level has been exceeded.

Clearance indicator for site reoccupation

5.29   The analytical sensitivity based on one half fibre counted in 200 graticules for a sample volume of air equivalent to at least 480 litres passed through a filter with an effective diameter greater than 20 mm is of the order of 0.0003 f/ml. However, due to background count levels on filters the limit of detection is 0.003 f/ml and the limit of quantification of the method is set at 0.010 f/ml, equivalent to a count of 40 fibre ends. In most cases it is reasonably practical to clean the working area following asbestos removal/remediation thoroughly enough for the respirable airborne fibre concentration to be below the limit of quantification after final cleaning, using the approved measuring method. Therefore a value of 0.010 fibres/ml is taken as the 'clearance indicator' threshold. This value is also used in the interpretation of reassurance and background samples.

5.30   The value calculated from each sample taken during site clearance testing should be compared with the clearance indicator value. At least 80% of the results should be less than 0.010 f/ml and all should be less than 0.015 f/ml. Thus, in smaller enclosures requiring four or fewer samples, all should be less than 0.010 f/ml, but in larger enclosures one result in five may lie between 0.010 f/ml and 0.015 f/ml. See Box 5.3 for an example.

5.31   The concentration value must be **calculated** correct to 3 decimal places to distinguish between 0.009 f/ml (which is acceptable) and 0.010 f/ml, which is unacceptable. The recommended reporting procedure, however, is as follows:

Calculated value	Report result as:
▪ Value ≤ 0.010 f/ml	<0.01 f/ml
▪ $0.010 \leq$ value ≤ 0.015	result to 3 decimal places
▪ Value ≥ 0.015 f/ml	result to 2 decimal places

6 Site assessment for reoccupation

6.1   Following asbestos removal, the premises must be assessed to determine whether they are thoroughly clean and fit for reoccupation (or, as appropriate, demolition). Once the licensed contractor is satisfied that the area is clean and ready for future use, the area should be assessed by an independent organisation which is accredited by UKAS as complying with ISO 17025.[20] All air measurements should comply with the ISO 17025 standard. If this assessment of the workplace is passed as satisfactory, then a certificate of reoccupation is issued. The certificate is issued to the contractor and, as appropriate, to the client where the latter has engaged the analyst.

6.2   The clearance certification process is a vital component in asbestos removal work. The issue of a certificate of reoccupation by an impartial and competent organisation provides the crucial reassurance and security to the subsequent building users. The multi-stage certification process is designed to allow the inspection and assessment to be performed in a structured, systematic and consistent manner. The contractor should not arrange for the site clearance certification procedure to start until satisfied that the area is clean and dry.

6.3   The analyst and the contractor need to co-operate and support each other during this process. Each also needs to understand the respective roles and responsibilities. It is the responsibility of the contractor to thoroughly and diligently clean up the work area. The analyst's role is to provide independent verification that the area is clean and suitable for subsequent use. It is not the analyst's role to oversee the final clean of the area. It is the analyst's role during clearance certification to direct the contractor to those matters which require attention to ensure successful completion of the process. The analyst should allow sufficient time for clearance certification to be performed.

6.4   There are four stages to the site certification for reoccupation procedure:

Stage 1: Preliminary check of site condition and job completeness;
Stage 2: A thorough visual inspection inside the enclosure/work area;
Stage 3: Air monitoring;
Stage 4: Final assessment post-enclosure/work area dismantling.

Stage 1: Preliminary check of site condition and job completeness

6.5   Initially the analyst needs to establish with the contractor the scope of the work that has been carried out. This must be done by examining the plan of work (see *Asbestos: The licensed contractors' guide*, Chapter 2).[3] Regulation 7(2) of CAWR[10] states that the plan of work should be kept at the premises until the work is completed. Paragraph 38 of the CAWR ACOP (L28)[12] states that the plan of work should be brought to the attention of anyone carrying out the four-stage certification procedure. It should be clear from the plan of work:

■   where the asbestos to be removed was;
■   if any asbestos materials were to remain in situ; and
■   what the asbestos materials removed were.

6.6   The HSE's Asbestos Licensing Unit has provided guidance to contractors on what should be contained in the plan of work. It should include, among other things, a diagram indicating the layout of the site and what asbestos is to be removed. If there is no plan of work on site or if the contractor refuses to make it available, **the inspection should either stop until such time as a plan of work is made available or a 'failed' certificate of reoccupation issued with the reason for the failure noted.**

(a)

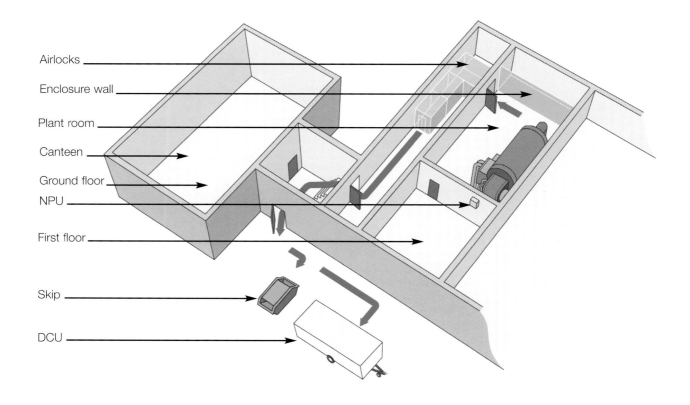

(b)

Figure 6.1 Recording of the site layout as a diagram, (a) shows the 3-dimensional layout and (b) is an example of how the site could be recorded as a clearance diagram. Dark areas show work areas and light areas show other areas which need to be inspected

6.7   A diagram or photos should be appended to the site certificate for reoccupation so that the scope of the work is quite clear. A copy of the diagram from the contractor's plan of work would meet this requirement. If there is no diagram on site, the analyst should prepare a diagram. The diagram should contain the main features. It should show the enclosure (or work area) including airlocks and baglocks, transit and waste routes, and skip and hygiene facilities. It should provide details of sizes or dimensions. An example of a diagram is shown in Figure 6.1. The analyst and contractor should agree the content of the diagram and both should sign and date it.

6.8   When the scope of the work has been understood and verified, the analyst should ensure that the hygiene facilities are still intact, operational and clean. The clean end of the unit should be checked for cleanliness, hot and cold water and heating. The shower area and dirty end should be inspected either by external viewing (from the clean end in the case of the former) or by entering wearing the appropriate RPE and PPE. These areas should be clean and free from stored items and the negative pressure unit should be operating. The analyst should then check the surrounding areas to the enclosure including the transit and waste routes, and the areas immediately adjacent to the enclosure. The purpose of this inspection is to check for obvious signs of contamination arising from the work; either through leaks in the enclosure, burst waste bags or debris from inadequate decontamination procedures. This inspection does not require the detailed visual examination which is necessary inside the enclosure or work area.

Box 6.1 Multi-job sites

Where there are several jobs ongoing at the same site, using, for example, the same waste skip, it will not be possible for a Stage 1 inspection to be carried out in that area, as it is still being used. In this case the Stage 1 certificate should state why that area has not been inspected and clearly identify the area that has been inspected. This principle would apply wherever there are common areas still in use on another job. The important thing is to be transparent; record the issue/problem and the steps taken by you to accommodate the situation on the certificate of reoccupation.

6.9   The integrity of the enclosure should also be checked. If any asbestos debris is found in the surrounding areas it should be cleared up immediately by the contractors. Any breach in the integrity of the enclosure should be repaired before Stage 2 is started. The analyst should make sure that the air extraction equipment is in situ and in operation. Air extraction equipment should be switched off just before starting the Stage 3 air monitoring and should not be removed until the third stage of the site certification procedure has been completed and the enclosure is being dismantled. The pre-filters on the air extraction equipment should be replaced with new ones before the final clean by the contractors.

Box 6.2 Conditions where an inspection of the transit routes should take place

Conditions should allow the identification of obvious asbestos debris along transit and waste routes. Under normal circumstances, rain or damp ground should not prevent a Stage 1 inspection as the analyst is looking for visible debris, not fine settled dust. An inspection at night would not be a problem if the routes were well-lit. If, however, the analyst felt that conditions did not allow reasonable inspection, eg insufficient light, then it should be delayed until the conditions are suitable, eg the following day. In the very rare occurrences where a delay is likely to be significant, eg several days (eg due to snow covering), then the analyst should record the situation in the certificate of reoccupation and continue with the remaining clearance stages. The certificate of reoccupation should be issued as appropriate. However, the analyst and the contractor will have to return and complete Stage 1 (and Stage 4 if appropriate) as soon as possible after the conditions allow. The ACOP provides for this variation from the norm in paragraph 157, where it states 'Site clearance certification should **normally** be carried out in four successive stages, with the next stage only being commenced when the previous one has been completed.'

If transit and waste routes are strewn with debris that could be mistaken for asbestos, or such that it is difficult to inspect for debris, the analyst should request that the routes be cleared to allow for adequate inspection.

The inspection is for obvious asbestos contamination and debris, not any other kind of debris.

6.10   The analyst should examine the enclosure through the viewing panels before entering in order to gain an initial impression of the job completeness. Items to look out for include:

- waste remaining in the enclosure;
- visible debris on the surfaces;
- inadequate lighting to conduct a visual inspection;
- essential equipment such as ladders or scaffolding are still present so it is possible to inspect all areas;
- puddles of water, wet patches and leaking pipes;
- evidence that sealant has been applied to exposed surfaces;
- potential hazards inside the enclosure.

6.11   If any of these items need to be actioned, they should be dealt with before the enclosure is entered. The analyst should direct the contractor to the matters needing to be rectified. The analyst should also discuss with the contractor if any of the items were identified in the plan of work as needing special attention (eg ingress of water). The type of action needed to overcome these problems is given in paragraphs 6.22-6.29. The analyst must make a formal record of the scenarios encountered and the discussions and actions that took place to rectify them. If viewing panels are either absent (eg have not been possible or have not been provided) or are insufficient (ie do not allow views of all of the work area), a note of this should be made in the analyst's site record and the above items considered when entering the enclosure in Stage 2.

There is no point entering the enclosure until these problems have been rectified

6.12   Findings at Stage 1 should be recorded on the certificate of reoccupation and verified with the contractor before moving on to the second stage. There should be confirmation that the plan of work has been inspected and that the air extraction equipment, hygiene facilities and work areas are intact and operating. This stage should also contain a record of findings of the inspection of the skip/waste route, the transit route, hygiene facilities and the outside of the enclosure. See Appendix 3. A note should be made of any remaining asbestos that was outside the scope of the work.

6.13   Only when the analyst is satisfied with the Stage 1 inspection, should he/she enter the enclosure to carry out the Stage 2 inspection. The analyst should generally be entering an area that is free of all asbestos and should not normally be expected to have to undergo full decontamination on exiting the enclosure. However, if the site is found to have extensive debris and surface contamination remaining, it is important that the analyst terminates the Stage 2 visual inspection and leaves the enclosure before any significant disturbance or clean-up takes place. Failure to do this will mean the analyst could be contaminated by the contractors' activity and will need to follow full decontamination procedures on leaving the enclosure (see Chapter 9 on decontamination).

Stage 2: Thorough visual inspection

6.14   This is the stage at which the thorough visual inspection of the enclosure or work area takes place. It is the most significant part of the clearance procedure. The analyst must check:

- the completeness of the removal of the ACMs from the underlying surfaces;
- for the presence of any visible asbestos debris left inside the enclosure and airlocks or work area;
- for the presence of fine settled dust.

6.15   The removal process will have given rise to the spread of asbestos dust inside the enclosure. Residual dust may still remain on any unprotected or inadequately cleaned surfaces. Such dust presents an ongoing risk to building occupants. Therefore a thorough visual examination of all surfaces should be performed. It should involve a close and detailed inspection across all parts of the enclosure kneeling down or using ladders where appropriate (see Figure 6.2). All items should be checked. The inspection can be assisted by using a torch and by running a fingertip across the surfaces to check for presence of fine dust (see Figure 6.3). Awkward or difficult locations must not be excluded. Baglocks and airlocks should be included.

Figure 6.2 Analyst carrying out a visual inspection inside an enclosure

6.16   The analyst should be accompanied during the thorough visual inspection by a representative of the contractor, who can rectify any minor problems found, such as:

- holes in the enclosure not visible from the outside;
- small amounts of dust or debris found during the course of the inspection.

6.17   The analyst will have to make judgements on the extent and significance of dust and debris found during the inspection: whether it is minor and can be cleaned up during the course of the inspection, or whether it is more substantial and is indicative that the final clean has not been undertaken thoroughly enough. It is important to remember that it is the duty of the contractor to undertake the final clean and carry out a thorough visual inspection before requesting a four-stage site certification for reoccupation. If it is clear that this has not been done, the analyst should withdraw and fail the enclosure, citing what needs to be done before another inspection is undertaken. The risk that the analyst undertaking an inspection will miss some contamination is increased if he/she has to stop and get cleaning done every few minutes. They should withdraw and let the contractors clean and re-inspect before starting a new visual inspection.

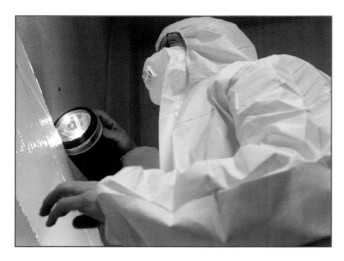

Figure 6.3 A torch being used to illuminate fine settled dust

6.18 Essential equipment to take into an enclosure includes:

- **a torch** – the torch beam when shone along a surface at a shallow angle is useful in identifying fine settled dust on surfaces; it can also augment the lighting in the enclosure;
- **a screwdriver** – this is useful for poking behind pipes and into crevices to help inspect these difficult-to-see areas;
- **a mirror** – this can be useful in inspecting difficult-to-see areas.

6.19 Locations where asbestos dust and debris are commonly found during thorough visual inspections are shown in Figure 6.4. Asbestos dust and debris may also be found in the folds of sheeting used to construct the enclosure.

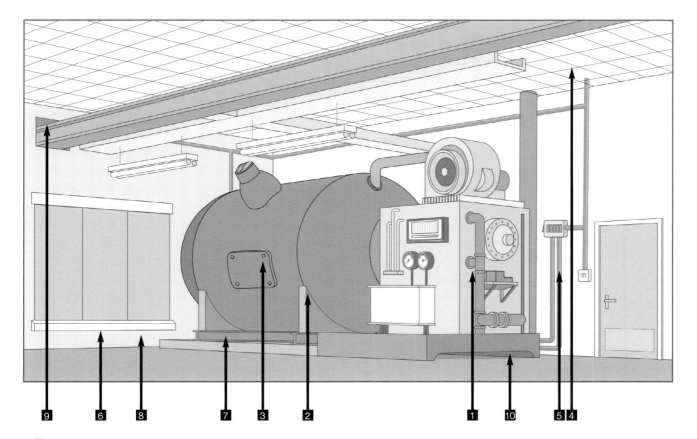

1	Backs of pipes and vessels
2	Support brackets and clamps on pipes and vessels
3	Nuts and bolts or flanges and hatches of vessels and pipework
4	Screw holes, or around nails and battens for AIB tiling
5	Cable trays and conduits, especially if they have a metal mesh construction
6	All horizontal ledges, shelves, window sills etc
7	The undersides of boilers and tanks, either attached or loose
8	Rough porous brickwork, eg breeze block and rough concrete
9	Holes in walls etc, where pipes, cables or steelwork pass through
10	Drains, sumps and culverts

Figure 6.4 Boiler room showing locations where asbestos dust and debris are commonly found during a thorough visual inspection

6.20   Equipment that must remain in the enclosure to help inspection includes:

■   stepladders/scaffolding – depending on the height of the enclosure one or other will be needed to allow safe access and to inspect the ledges, pipework etc above head height;

■   lighting – a thorough inspection needs lighting; a torch alone is not enough. The torch should be used to supplement the background lighting, not replace it;

■   vacuum cleaner and other cleaning materials – this will allow the contractor to clean any minor amounts of debris identified by the analyst immediately; a vacuum cleaner must also be available for preliminary decontamination on leaving the enclosure;

■   buckets of water and sponges and brushes or wipes in the airlock to aid preliminary decontamination, following the visual inspection.

How long should a visual inspection take?

6.21   The analyst must ensure that sufficient time is available for the visual inspection. A detailed visual inspection can be time-consuming, and the length of time needed will depend on the size and complexity of the job. A thorough visual search of all areas of the enclosure is required to be confident that an area is clean and free from asbestos debris and fine settled dust. A single panel removed from behind a domestic boiler within a 2 m^2 enclosure with smooth surfaces and nothing else within the enclosure is unlikely to take more than 10-15 minutes. Even a small boiler house should not take less than about 1.5 hours if inspected thoroughly. A large plant room, chemical plant or power station may take several days. During a large clearance, analysts should leave the enclosure, decontaminate and take a break every 2-3 hours. The time spent carrying out a visual inspection should be recorded.

Problems commonly encountered during visual inspections

6.22   Paragraphs 6.22–6.29 provide guidance on several issues which may be encountered during visual inspections. Potential problems can arise due to insufficient planning and preparation. Clearance should be considered by the contractor at the very outset of the job. There is a requirement for the contractor to consider clearance in the initial assessment of the work (ACOP L28[12] paragraph 30). The contractor should be looking to identify those matters which will inhibit or impede clearance, eg wet enclosures, loose or naturally dusty surfaces, voids in ceilings which contain mineral wool, congested plant rooms which contain multiple pipes or equipment. These matters can normally be eliminated or resolved more easily before the work starts.

Wet enclosures
6.23   This is a problem commonly cited by analysts when undertaking clearances. The ACOP L28[12] states that an enclosure, where practical, should be clean and dry. However, the enclosure is sometimes wet. There are a variety of reasons for this: there may be a leaking pipe; sealant may have been sprayed in the enclosure; or there may be groundwater seeping through. If groundwater is

present there may be little that can be done to render the enclosure completely dry, but it may be necessary for the contractor to use a pump to prevent the area flooding. However if there is a leaking pipe, there are two scenarios:

■   If it is identified before work is carried out, it can be pointed out to the client and fixed before work begins. It can also be explained to the asbestos removal contractors that they will be unable to obtain a certificate of reoccupation if the leak is not fixed. If the situation is further complicated by the fact that the pipe is lagged with asbestos, then a preliminary removal job can be carried out. A small enclosure should be built and a section of lagging removed using a glove bag. This will allow plumbers to carry out their work once the area has obtained a certificate of reoccupation.

■   If the leak is identified during the course of the work, work should cease and the area cleaned. The plumber can then be accompanied into the enclosure by the contractor. The air extraction system should stay on. Plumbers should have suitable training in the use of the RPE and PPE to allow them to carry out their work safely. A leaking pipe should be no excuse for a wet enclosure. **An enclosure will fail a visual examination if it is wet and the cause is remediable.**

Sprayed sealant
6.24   Paragraph 161 of the L28[12] ACOP also states that sealants should not be sprayed before a visual inspection or disturbed air tests. The only exception to this is where there is sufficient non-asbestos dust (eg from concrete) to cause a failure in the air test. The analyst has discretionary powers and, after due consideration and air testing, can allow sealant to be used in these circumstances (see paragraph 6.34 of this guidance). The circumstances should be recorded on the certificate of reoccupation and the air test should proceed. If an analyst arrives on site to carry out a visual inspection and the enclosure is still wet due to sealant being sprayed, the analyst must fail the area and inform the contractor that the Stage 2 inspection can only be carried out when the sealant has been washed off and the enclosure is dry. If the sealant has already dried the analyst will have to fail the site and consider the way forward. If the evidence suggests that the sealant is protecting a significant amount of asbestos dust which will cause risk to subsequent occupants, then the sealant will have to be removed and the area recleaned. The client should be informed.

Enclosures with loose rubble flooring
6.25   The assessment should identify work areas where the flooring is loose rubble, eg in an undercroft. In these circumstances the rubble should be removed (to a specified depth) as part of a pre-clean of the site. The loose flooring would then be sealed with an impervious layer, eg metal or hardboard sheeting, before the asbestos work begins. If it was not possible to remove the rubble due to the condition of the remaining ACM or space limitations, then the matter should be addressed in the assessment. The plan of work should identify the procedure to remove the rubble and loose soil after the ACM removal has been carried out. In these circumstances, it would be prudent for the contractor to consult with the analyst before starting the work. If an

analyst arrives on site to carry out the four-stage clearance certification, without prior discussion and agreement of the procedures for clearance, it will be impossible to pass such an area according to the standard required in a Stage 2 inspection. The analyst will have to fail the site and liaise with the contractor and/or client to organise the removal of a specified depth of the rubble/loose flooring before the formal inspection begins. The depth of rubble to be removed will depend on the level of contamination. The analyst can then check the remaining flooring for signs of asbestos contamination. If the analyst is satisfied that the contamination has been removed, the flooring can then be sealed and Stage 2 visual can formally start.

Figure 6.5 Remnants of asbestos on breeze blocks

Asbestos remaining in enclosures (by design)
6.26   There may be occasions when some asbestos is to remain in situ in the enclosure. It may be that only damaged asbestos lagging is being removed from pipe work, and that undamaged material is to remain; or it could be that asbestos ceiling tiles are being removed, but a fire door with an asbestos cement panel is being left in place. In these circumstances the ACM should be labelled that it is asbestos and that it is to remain. The item can then be checked by the analyst against the work plan and recorded on the certificate of reoccupation.

Asbestos waste remaining in enclosure
6.27   On occasions, it may be necessary to retain asbestos waste (bagged or wrapped) within the enclosure until Stage 4 of clearance certification starts and the enclosure can be removed. This situation may arise when oversized waste (such as lengths of pipe work or large AIB panels) cannot be removed through the baglock system. The items should remain in the enclosure and be subject to inspection along with other items to make sure they are free of asbestos debris on the outside of the wrapping. The items will also need to be moved to allow the analyst to inspect the underlying surfaces.

Inaccessible asbestos
6.28   Where asbestos has been spray applied, there are often crevices or holes through walls where pipe work or girders run. These may contain asbestos but are impossible to clean so that all asbestos is removed. In these cases, the analyst may permit the use of non-flammable sealant such as foams or plaster to fill the hole and seal the asbestos within it. However, the analyst should be satisfied that as far as reasonably practicable, the asbestos has been removed before the sealant is applied. The client for the contract (eg building occupier) should be informed that this is the proposed course of action before the encapsulation takes place. It should be in the plan of work. The location of the sealant and remaining asbestos should be noted on the certificate of reoccupation, so that the client can record the presence of the asbestos in the management plan. If an analyst arrives on site to find that holes around the area where the sprayed asbestos was applied have been plugged with foam or other sealant, the contractor should be instructed to remove the sealant before the Stage 2 inspection begins.

Use of encapsulant and sealant
6.29   Where asbestos has been sprayed onto porous surfaces (eg breeze blocks) or onto tar, it is almost

impossible to remove all the asbestos, sufficient to pass a visual inspection (see Figure 6.5). In these cases the analysts, having satisfied themselves that further removal is not reasonably practicable, should advise the contractor and/or client to seal the residual asbestos with a permanent proprietary sealant. The visual inspection can then begin again once the sealant has been applied and dried. Encapsulation of asbestos in these instances should not take place before the analyst has seen the residual asbestos.

6.30   The findings of Stage 2 of the inspection should be recorded on the certificate of reoccupation. There should be confirmation that the airlocks and enclosure are free from visible debris and contamination, that all ACMs have been removed and that the interior surfaces of the enclosure are free from visible debris and settled dust. See Appendix 3. As for Stage 1, if problems are encountered during the Stage 2 inspection, the analyst must make a formal record of the scenarios encountered and the discussions and actions that took place to rectify them. The analyst should also make specific comments on the certificate of reoccupation if any asbestos is to remain (see paragraphs 6.28-6.29) and clearly identify the locations of these areas with a recommendation that this information should be entered into the management plan/asbestos register.

Stage 3: Clearance indicator air sampling for the certificate of reoccupation

6.31   Air sampling takes place once a thorough visual inspection has been carried out and the analyst is satisfied that all the asbestos in the plan of work has been removed, and there is no visible debris or layers of settled dust (see Figure 6.6). The lowest airborne respirable asbestos concentration that the method described in Appendix 1 and MDHS 39/4 can reliably quantify is 0.01 fibres/ml, for a sample volume of at least 480 litres passed through a filter with an effective diameter greater than 20 mm. In most cases it is reasonably practicable to clean the working area thoroughly enough for the respirable airborne fibre concentration after final cleaning to be below that limit, using the approved measuring method. Therefore a value of 0.01 fibres/ml is taken as the 'clearance indicator' threshold, and a site should not normally be regarded as fit for reoccupation until the asbestos in air measurements are below this level.

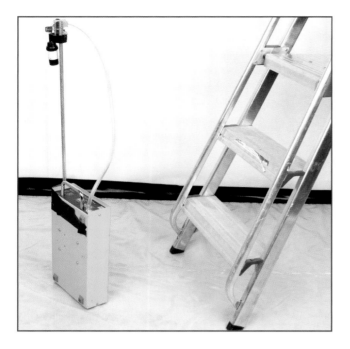

Figure 6.6 Air sampling during clearance

6.32   Details of the equipment to be used to carry out the sampling and analysis are given in Appendix 1 and MDHS 39/4. The strategy for sampling and dust disturbance is given in paragraphs 5.15-5.19. The detailed analysis of the filters collected is also given in Appendix 1. Air sampling should be accompanied by sweeping the floor with a broom and brushing the surface from which the asbestos was removed and any other higher level horizontal surfaces (see Figure 6.7). Brushing should also take place on horizontal surfaces where the dust may have settled or collected or where there is suspicion of surface contamination, and on surfaces in close proximity to the sampling equipment. The broom and/or brush used should be made out of man-made fibre and should be used to give a representative simulation of cleaning activity. For enclosures with floor areas >20 m² a long-handled broom should be used to sweep the floor, for both ergonomic and practical reasons.

6.33   The dust disturbance should be carried out as described in paragraphs 5.15-5.19. The dust-raising activities undertaken and their duration should be recorded on the certificate of reoccupation. See Appendix 3. On some surfaces, brushing may generate significant amounts of particulate which may obscure the filter. If this is the case sampling strategies may need to be modified to take this into account (see paragraph 6.31). Appropriate PPE should be worn by the person conducting the disturbance test (see Chapter 8).

Dusty enclosures

6.34   There may be occasions when the surface in the work area is a source of non-asbestos dust that would generate unreadable filters. The presence of non-asbestos dust would be noted at the thorough visual inspection. The analyst has to be satisfied that the dust is non-asbestos. However, the analyst should proceed with air sampling as normal. If this produces unreadable filters, the analyst should

Figure 6.7 Analyst carrying out disturbance by brushing during clearance

consider sampling for shorter periods with paired samplers, so that the dust loading on each filter is reduced. If the samples fail again because of the dust loading, then the spraying of surfaces with a sealant should be considered. If a sealant is used, the air test should not be carried out until the sealant is dry (see paragraph 6.24).

Assessment of air sampling results

6.35   After air sampling, the analyst will check the final flow rate and collect samples for phase contrast microscopy analysis. The analyst will count the fibres in a minimum of 200 graticule areas and report the calculated fibre concentrations for each sample (see paragraphs 5.28-5.30). The analyst will also produce a clear statement whether the enclosure has passed or failed, relative to the clearance indicator value (0.01 f/ml) (see Appendix 3).

Leaks in enclosures

6.36   Under normal circumstances, the air extraction equipment should be turned off and capped during the air test. The analyst should check that the pre-filter was changed before the final clean. However, if, in the opinion of the analyst, switching the air extraction system off would compromise the integrity of the enclosure, **and** there are people near the enclosure who may be exposed to airborne asbestos fibres above the clearance indicator as a consequence, the analyst can direct the contractors to leave the system switched on during the air test. Any decision to leave the air extraction system switched on should be recorded, with reasons why, on the certificate of reoccupation.

Stage 4: Final assessment post-enclosure/work area dismantling

6.37   Once the enclosure (or work area) has passed the visual inspection (Stage 2) and air monitoring (Stage 3), the enclosure can be dismantled. Under normal circumstances the analyst will probably remain on site during dismantling (unless the deconstruction is not to take place for some time). If the analyst is close to the dismantling work, appropriate PPE should be worn as trapped pockets of asbestos could be released during the physical disturbance. Reassurance sampling could be carried out during the dismantling procedure to check for any release of airborne asbestos. After the enclosure has been removed, the analyst should visually inspect the area to ensure it is clean. At this stage the analyst is looking for obvious asbestos debris such as from the sheeting of the enclosure as it was dismantled or from debris which has been missed during cleaning. The analyst should also re-inspect the waste route and transit route for asbestos debris.

6.38   Where there is some debris, this can be cleaned by the contractor's employees, wearing appropriate PPE including RPE, immediately using a type H vacuum and wiped with a wet disposable cloth. If the area is too contaminated to allow immediate cleaning without the prospect of spreading contamination, the site should be failed, re-enclosed, re-cleaned, and the visual inspection and disturbed air test repeated.

6.39   If there are fuse boxes or switches within the area and the analyst suspects they may be contaminated, a qualified electrician should be made available to isolate the boxes, so they can be inspected.

6.40   The analyst should record what has been inspected, what was found and the outcome on the certificate of reoccupation. See Appendix 3.

Certificate of reoccupation

6.41   Once all four stages of the clearance procedure have been completed satisfactorily, the analyst should issue a certificate of reoccupation. Each stage of the certification should have been completed in sequence, to ensure that the information included is as complete as possible. The information should be clear and unambiguous so all parties know the scope and extent of clearance and any particular matters which have been dealt with.

6.42   A template for a certificate of reoccupation setting out the details it should contain can be found in Appendix 3. If one of the stages fails, the reasons for the failure should be entered and the remaining stages struck through. A signed acknowledgement of the failure should be obtained from the contractor's site representative (usually the site supervisor). If the failure occurs at either Stage 1 or 2 of the process, the inspections (both Stage 1 and Stage 2) will need to be repeated. If a new analyst carries out the work, the whole procedure should start again. If the site fails at Stage 3 or 4, it is only necessary to repeat these stages until both have passed. The analyst will then need to cross-refer

to, and append the certificate where the Stages 1 and 2 were passed. It is very important that the contractor's representative acknowledges the outcome on each certificate issued, whether for a pass or a failure, as this provides evidence of when the outcome was communicated. The certificate will provide documentary evidence of the work undertaken by the analyst and should be retained by the analyst. Copies of each certificate must be issued to the contractor and, as necessary, to the client employing the analyst. This may be done after the analyst has left the site, provided the contractor's representative has acknowledged the outcome. Each certificate should bear a unique number.

Inspection certificate for the hygiene facilities

6.43   Once the certificate of reoccupation has been issued, the analyst can begin the clearance of the hygiene facility. This should be inspected and air tested. The air test should be accompanied by disturbance of surfaces in the dirty and shower areas. Obviously there is no requirement for a four-stage certification procedure here, as Stages 1 and 4 are carried out as part of the main certification for reoccupation. Only Stages 2 and 3 of the procedure are required.

6.44   The hygiene facility should be clean and dry before the inspection takes place and any potentially asbestos-contaminated materials removed (eg bags containing used coveralls, used/discarded respirator filters, transit clothing). It is recommended that the unit is entered through the clean end to check that this area is clean and free of bagged materials, before carrying out a detailed clearance in the shower area and dirty end. The clearance should be carried out using the same criteria as for enclosures. If the inspection shows that no dust and debris are present, clearance air sampling should be carried out in the shower area and dirty end. For very small units where the combined floor area of the shower and dirty areas is <10 m^2, one air test is sufficient if the door between the shower and dirty areas is propped open and the sample head is positioned in the doorway. Where the combined floor area of the shower and dirty end exceeds 10 m^2, a sample in each of the shower and dirty areas should be taken. A minimum air volume of 480 litres should be sampled for each sample. During air sampling, the extraction in the hygiene facility should be switched off and capped and surface disturbance should be carried out using a brush for 1.5 minutes for each sample. A separate inspection certificate (see Appendix 4) should be issued for the hygiene facility. The hygiene facility should normally be subjected to the inspection and air sampling before it is moved off-site (see paragraph 6.45). The analyst should review with the contractor whether or not the hygiene facility is to remain on site following the issue of the inspection certificate and a note of this made on the certificate.

6.45   Where, for security reasons, hygiene facilities are not left on site overnight, inspection certification is not required until the end of the contract. In these situations, information on where the hygiene facility is to be stored overnight and other arrangements should be included in the plan of work sent to HSE with the ASB5 notification. Further information on this can be found in *Asbestos: The licensed contractors' guide*.[3]

7 Supervisory work carried out by analysts

7.1   Some analytical consultancies carry out management and/or supervisory work on asbestos contracts for clients. This may range from witnessing a smoke test and carrying out leakage testing during the period of the removal work, through to a full management service including drawing up specifications for tender packages and reviewing quotations and supervising the contractors.

7.2   Analysts offering a management service may require a supervisory licence from HSE's Asbestos Licensing Unit. In order to obtain a supervisory licence, analysts will have to have completed relevant training (see paragraph 3.9). The following paragraphs clarify when such a licence is required.

7.3   Regulation 2 of the ASLIC Regulations 1983[13] states that *'work with asbestos insulation or asbestos coating or asbestos insulating board'* means:

(a)   *work which consists of the removal, repair or disturbance of asbestos insulation or asbestos coating or asbestos insulating board;*
(b)   *work which is ancillary to such work; and*
(c)   *supervising work referred to subparagraphs (a) or (b) above.*

7.4   The guidance to the ASLIC Regulations goes on to state in paragraph 18 that *'work carried out in a supervisory capacity requires a licence. This means work involving direct supervisory control over those removing, repairing or disturbing asbestos.'* Direct supervisory control over asbestos work will include supervising ancillary work and all work associated with (and necessary for) work with asbestos. Direct supervisory work may involve entry into enclosures, as well as covering the external situations.

7.5   There is no legal requirement to have a supervisory licence holder (SLH) on site but if an analyst is performing SLH duties on site, they must hold a licence.

7.6   Direct supervisory control is taken to mean where there is direct and immediate influence over current site activities including:

■   any aspect of the work with asbestos including the equipment and controls being used;
■   how the work is done, eg methods, techniques etc;
■   how the site is prepared, cleaned up etc;
■   the monitoring of controls, eg inspecting hygiene units, changing pre-filters on the air extraction system etc;
■   movement, storage and transfer of waste.

7.7   A supervisory licence is not required if you are:

■   the client who has engaged the contractor doing the work;
■   the principal contractor and the work with asbestos is being done by a sub-contractor;
■   an analyst carrying out work for the certificate of reoccupation or an inspection certificate at the end of the job;
■   carrying out quality control work, eg air monitoring outside enclosures or checking that the work has been carried out to the agreed standard;
■   a consultant or other preparing the method statement; or
■   a consultant or other reviewing tender submissions on behalf of the client.

7.8   During supervisory work, the supervisor must control exposure to asbestos to as low as reasonably practicable. Some supervisory work can be carried out from outside the live enclosure, but this requires there to be sufficient, well-placed viewing panels, which allow the supervisor to view what is going on. The size of the enclosure, the distance between the asbestos removal and viewing panels, the line of sight, the number of removal operatives inside the enclosure and the complexity of the job will determine how much time will be spent inside the enclosure. Viewing panels can be used to check that:

■   PPE and other safety procedures are being used correctly;
■   wet removal methods are being properly and consistently employed;
■   asbestos debris is being minimised by placing the removed material directly into sacks and cleaning up material on the floor on a regular basis;
■   measurements are being carried out to ensure the asbestos material is adequately wet (eg moisture readings, colour change and squeeze testing samples before removal);
■   bags of waste only contain wet ACMs (if necessary waste bags can be taken from the skip and reopened inside the enclosure in front of the viewing panel);
■   inspecting the pre-filters from the air extraction system for the amount of dust collected before they are double bagged.

Reporting procedures

7.9   Where there is a management contract, the SLH, client and contractor must be very clear about the extent of responsibilities and the lines of reporting. It is recommended that the contract drawn up between the client and the contractor specifies the role the SLH will play in the management of the asbestos contract. The contract between the client and the SLH should also be specific. Both the contractor and the SLH should be clear on their responsibilities. Each party should be clear on who is responsible for:

■   the day-to-day management of the site;
■   conducting the smoke test;
■   conducting leak testing;
■   carrying out air sampling, inside and/or outside the enclosure with indication of numbers and frequency;
■   directly supervising the work activities of the contractors;
■   reassurance air tests during and/or after the removal of the enclosure.

The contract between the client and the SLH should also specify the following information:

■   a contact name for the SLH to report to;
■   how often the SLH is expected to report to the client contact;
■   what the SLH is expected to report to the client;
■   the time frame in which the work is to be completed;
■   at what times is there expected to be an SLH on site;
■   arrangements for emergency call-outs out of hours; and
■   any penalty clauses.

8 Personal protective equipment

8.1 This section explains personal protective equipment (PPE), in particular respiratory protective equipment (RPE), its provision, use and maintenance.

Respiratory protective equipment

8.2 The exact level of exposure that causes asbestos-related diseases is unclear. But we do know the more asbestos fibres breathed in, the greater the risk to health. That is why it is important that everyone who works with asbestos should take the strictest precautions to reduce exposure to asbestos fibres as low as reasonably practicable and in any case to a concentration which is below the relevant control limits. This will include choosing the right RPE for the job, checking that it is fitted correctly before each use and ensuring it is maintained in good condition.

Figure 8.1 Fit checking of RPE

Box 8.1 Fit checking of RPE

Respiratory protective equipment will only provide the expected level of protection to the user if, each time it is worn, care is taken to fit the respirator so that an effective seal is formed between the face and the seal. Each time the respirator is worn, the fit should be checked following the manufacturers' instructions. This usually involves adjusting the strap position and tension (and the nose seals of disposable respirators) before blocking off the filter and inhaling strongly to create a negative pressure inside the respirator (see Figure 8.1). The mask should collapse inwards. If any leakage is detected, adjust the position of the mask, and/or the tension of the straps. Retest. If a seal cannot be obtained, do not use this mask.

8.3   CAWR 2002[10] requires employers to do all that is reasonably practicable to prevent exposure to asbestos fibres, or where prevention is not possible, to reduce exposure to as low as reasonably practicable. In addition, employers must always provide suitable RPE if, despite the precautions taken, exposure to asbestos fibres is liable to exceed the 'control limits' laid down in the Regulations.

8.4   It is generally unlikely that the analyst will be exposed to airborne asbestos fibres at concentrations above the control limits unless they enter a 'live' asbestos enclosure for supervisory purposes. However, situations where the asbestos is being actively disturbed by the analyst (eg during disturbance brushing for the certificate of reoccupation and during the collection of samples of asbestos materials) will also have the potential to give raised airborne fibre levels. Much can be done to prevent entry into a live enclosure being necessary (see paragraph 7.8).

8.5   Also, as part of the preliminary check of job completeness in the four-stage site certification procedure, the analyst should examine the enclosure through the viewing panel to ascertain that it is ready for inspection. If the area appears dirty or asbestos debris can clearly be seen, the analyst should not enter the enclosure until it has been cleaned sufficiently.

CE-marking

8.6   The RPE used by analysts must be marked with a 'CE' symbol. This means it meets the minimum legal requirements, usually by conforming to a European Standard.

8.7   The RPE provided must also be suitable for the job.

Suitable RPE

8.8   The equipment will need to be matched to the type of work to be done, the working environment, the wearer, and the airborne fibre concentrations (expected or measured). This means it will need to:

- provide adequate protection (ie reduce the wearer's exposure to asbestos fibres to as low as is reasonably practicable, and anyway to below the control limits) during the job in hand and in the specified working environment (eg confined spaces);
- if fan-assisted, provide clean air at a flow rate and duration that conforms to the manufacturer's minimum specifications;
- if air-fed, provide clean air at a flow rate that at least conforms to the minimum recommended by the manufacturer;
- properly fit the wearer;
- be reasonably comfortable to wear;
- be properly maintained; and
- not introduce additional hazards that may put the wearer's health and safety at risk.

When choosing RPE you need to think about:

- the expected concentrations of asbestos fibres in the air;

- the protection factor values of different types of RPE (eg see Table 8.1);
- the potential for oxygen deficiency and/or the presence of other hazardous substances (eg solvent vapours) within the work environment. You should be aware that particulate filters used for protection against asbestos fibres will not protect against oxygen deficiency, gases or vapours. Work in oxygen-deficient atmospheres must comply with the requirements of the Confined Spaces Regulations 1997;[24]
- the kind of work involved;
- the temperatures at which people will be working;
- the facial characteristics of the wearers (eg beards, sideburn, glasses etc);
- the medical fitness of the people wearing the equipment;
- the length of time the person will have to wear the equipment;
- how comfortable it is and whether people will wear it correctly for the required length of time;
- whether the job involves extensive movements, restrictions and/or obstructions which need to be overcome while doing the job;
- the need to communicate verbally during work;
- the effects of other PPE and other accessories on RPE (eg unmatched goggles may affect the face seal provided by the face mask);
- jewellery or other adornments (eg piercing) worn by the wearer which may interfere with the fit of the face mask.

8.9   More details on these aspects can be found in the HSE publication HSG53 *Respiratory protective equipment at work: A practical guide*.[25]

Expected exposure concentrations

8.10   The level of expected exposure should be established in an assessment. The results from previous air monitoring can be used to assist the assessment. Most analysts will not be exposed to airborne concentrations above the control limits (see paragraph 8.4).

Protection factors

8.11   The assessment should identify adequate RPE, ie RPE which reduces exposure to below the control limit as far as reasonably practicable.

8.12   Table 8.1 lists various types of RPE. In the selection process, the RPE which has the highest assigned protection factor (APF) should be considered initially. Then consider whether this RPE is suited to the nature of the job, work-related factors, wearer's facial characteristics, medical fitness and comfort. Using this process, select the most suitable type of RPE for the job. The selection should also consider whether the chosen RPE will be adequate for any unexpected short-term high exposures. The reasons for selecting a particular type of RPE should be recorded in the risk assessment.

8.13   In practice analysts are likely to wear only a limited range of RPE. A disposable type is likely to be used for inspection, survey, sampling and clearance procedures; and a full facepiece powered respirator will be worn when entry into a live enclosure is necessary. In these situations FFP3 type and equipment with a P3 type of filter should be used respectively. However some people may prefer to use half-masks rather than disposable equipment, and powered hoods or blouses may be used in some circumstances in place of full facepiece powered equipment (see paragraph 8.21).

Face mask fit and testing

8.14   The performance of face masks depends on achieving a good contact between the wearer's skin and the face seal of the face mask. As people's faces have a range of shapes and sizes, it is unlikely that one particular type or size of RPE face mask will fit everyone. Inadequate fit will significantly reduce the protection provided to the wearer. To make sure that the selected face mask can provide adequate protection for the wearer, a fit test should be carried out. There are two types of fit test that can be carried out. These should not be confused with the fit check, a procedure to verify that a good seal has been obtained each time the respirator is used (see Box 8.1).

Qualitative fit testing

8.15   Qualitative fit testing is a simple pass/fail test based on the wearer's subjective assessment of the leakage, via the face seal region, of a test agent. These tests are relatively simple to perform and are suitable for half-mask and filtering facepiece (disposable) respirators. They are not suitable for full facepiece RPE.

Quantitative fit testing

8.16   Quantitative fit testing provides a numerical measure of the fit and generates a 'fit factor' number. These tests give an objective measure of face fit. They require specialised equipment and are more complicated to carry out than qualitative methods. These methods should be used for full facepiece RPE and can be used for half masks and disposable respirators.

8.17   Further details on RPE fit testing can be found in the HSE Information Document HSE282/28 *Fit testing of respiratory protective equipment facepieces*.[26] This can be downloaded from the HSE website.

8.18   To obtain an adequate performance at the workplace, the selected RPE must be worn correctly every time. The expected level of workplace protection provided by suitable RPE is shown by the APF values in Table 8.1.

8.19   A repeat fit test should be conducted where the wearer:

- is changing to a different model of RPE or different sized face mask;
- has undergone a significant (>10%) weight change since the last test;
- undergoes any substantial dental work;
- develops any facial changes (scars, moles etc) around the face seal area; or
- if your health and safety policy requires it. It is recommended that employers have a specific policy on frequency of repeat fit testing: for example every one or two years.

8.20   Remember that beards, sideburns or even a visible growth of stubble or wearing glasses will affect the face seal of tight-fitting face masks, which rely on a close contact between face and mask. Employees wearing tight-fitting RPE should be clean shaven.

8.21   For workers who cannot wear a tight-fitting facepiece, equipment that does not rely on a good face seal for protection should be provided, eg powered or air-supplied hoods and powered or air-supplied blouses. For those wearing glasses, a full face mask which permits the fixing of special frames inside the mask should be employed where appropriate.

Table 8.1 Respirator selection chart for protection against asbestos in air

Assigned Protection Factor (APF)	Filtering half-mask BS EN 149	Valved filtering half-mask BS EN 405	Filtering half-masks without inhalation valves BS EN 1827	Half-mask BS EN 140 and filter BS EN 143	Full-face mask BS EN 136 and filter BS EN 143	Powered hoods and filter BS EN 146 BS EN 12941	Power-assisted masks and filter BS EN 147 BS EN 12942
40					Mask + P3	TH3 hoods, blouses + P3	TM3 full-face mask + P3
20	FF P3	FF P3	FM P3	Mask + P3		TH2 All types of face-pieces + P3	TM2 All types of face-pieces + P3

Care, maintenance and testing of RPE

Looking after RPE

8.22   The RPE must be checked to ensure it is clean and in good working order before it is given to the wearer, and before it goes back into storage. Badly maintained RPE will not provide adequate protection and the wearer's health will be put at risk. Before use, checks should be made on:

■   the condition of the head harness and the facepiece, including the seal and visor;
■   the condition of the inhalation and exhalation valves, where fitted. For example, dirty, curled-up or cracked valves will not perform properly and will severely compromise the protection provided;
■   the condition of any threaded connectors and seals;
■   the condition and type of filter(s), that they are 'in-date' and fitted properly;
■   the battery charge/condition;
■   the airflow rate for power-assisted and powered respirators compared with the manufacturer's specification - before the device is used;
■   whether the RPE is complete and correctly assembled; and
■   any additional tests in accordance with the manufacturer's instructions.

8.23   In addition to the pre-use checks detailed above, all RPE (except the disposable type) should be more thoroughly examined and tested, by trained personnel, before it is issued to any wearer for the first time and at least once a month to make sure that it is working properly to its design specification. A record of inspection, examination, maintenance and defects remedied must be kept for five years. Only proprietary spare parts should be used.

8.24   The manufacturer of RPE will provide instructions on cleaning, maintenance and additional checks and tests. The procedures should be followed. After each use, RPE (except the disposable type) should be decontaminated, cleaned, disinfected and placed in suitable storage specifically provided for that purpose.

Do not modify any form of RPE without the knowledge and consent of the manufacturer

RPE training for analysts

8.25   Analysts should be given adequate instruction, information and training on the following:

■   how to fit and use the RPE correctly;
■   why RPE must be worn correctly and the importance of fit testing for the initial selection of suitable equipment and pre-use fit-checking each time it is worn;
■   why RPE should never be taken off and/or put down in a contaminated area, except in a medical emergency;

■   how to recognise a reduction in air flow and what to do if it happens;
■   why a particular type of RPE has been selected, and what it can and cannot do;
■   the manufacturer's instructions on the use and maintenance of the equipment;
■   how to clean and decontaminate oneself and how to clean contaminated RPE when leaving the work area; and
■   when not in use, where and how to store the RPE.

8.26   Analysts should also receive regular refresher training (at least once a year) on the use of RPE. **From an employer's point of view, don't assume that because your workers have worn RPE before, they will always use it properly.**

8.27   It should be standard practice for analysts to check that the RPE is in good working order before use and that it is fitted properly.

Some common misuses of RPE when working with asbestos

8.28   Examples given below indicate some of the very serious misuses of RPE. Misuses of this kind will always result in reduced protection and unnecessary, and preventable, exposures to asbestos fibres. These misuses invalidate the suitability of RPE and constitute a failure to comply with CAWR 2002.[10]

All types of RPE
■   Wearing of disposable respirators and half and full face masks by people with facial hair which prevents an adequate seal being achieved.
■   Wearing safety goggles that are not compatible with the disposable respirator or a half-mask. Incompatible goggles will prevent an adequate seal being achieved.
■   Failing to ensure that the RPE fits the wearer.
■   Working in a contaminated area while the respirator is left hanging around the neck.
■   Using the RPE if it is dirty, damaged or incomplete.
■   Failing to properly maintain the RPE.
■   Leave the mask lying around in the workplace – dust will get inside and the wearer will breathe it in the next time it is put on.

Disposable respirators
■   Wearing the respirator upside down.
■   Failing to adjust the nose clip to obtain a good face fit and face seal.
■   Not using the two head straps correctly to obtain a good fit.
■   Working in a contaminated area while the respirator is left hanging around the neck or placed on top of the head.

RPE with full face masks
■   Failing to adequately tighten all the head harness straps.
■   Wearing ordinary spectacles with a full face mask. There are special frames that can be fitted inside the mask which do not interfere with the face seal.
■   Wearing the head harness over the hood of the coverall - this can cause slippage of the mask and loss of the face seal.

- Failing to ensure that the correct filter is fitted in the filter housing, or that seals/O-rings are in place and correctly seated.
- Failing to ensure that filters are present in their housing.
- Failing to tighten the breathing hose to the face mask and filter housing.
- Failing to replace worn and distorted masks.
- Failing to test the voltage and capacity of batteries, and to replace inadequate ones.
- Keeping working if the fan stops or the flow rate falls – leave the work area immediately.

Other personal protective equipment

Coveralls

8.29   The following paragraphs provide guidance on the type of PPE that should be worn for different analyst activities. Coveralls should be worn by analysts whenever a risk assessment indicates there is a possibility of contamination with asbestos fibres. Disposable coveralls are favoured as there are few laundries now accepting asbestos-contaminated items for washing. It is also easier to double bag disposable overalls and dispose of them as asbestos waste either on site where there are facilities, or at base. Coverall material must be sufficiently strong and robust to withstand abrasive physical contact and damage from crawling, kneeling and climbing in the demanding environment of a removal site. The coveralls must also limit the penetration of fibres through intact material. Type 5 category 3 disposable coveralls provide an acceptable standard and should be used.

PPE for surveying
8.30   During Type 1 and some simple Type 2 surveys (eg no licensable ACMs involved) or other low risk situations, a coverall worn over normal clothing (and suitable RPE) should be sufficient. However, in other survey situations or where entry into dusty or potentially contaminated areas is expected, normal clothing should not be worn. In these situations the potential for contamination is greater and, if coverall protection is breached (eg through tearing), undergarments could become contaminated. In these circumstances arrangements should be made for decontamination, eg changing and showering, if necessary. It would be practical to wear two pairs of disposable coveralls, so that on completion of the work, the top coverall can be double bagged and disposed of as asbestos waste and the other coverall can be worn to the changing facilities.

8.31   Normal work wear shoes should be sufficient for most survey work. However, if working in areas where the potential for contamination is greater, such as during destructive Type 3 surveys or working in unpredictable spaces such as undercrofts, then laceless boots such as wellington boots would be suitable. These can easily be cleaned of any potential contamination.

8.32   Disposable gloves may also be worn in the above situation or when sampling suspected ACMs, to prevent contamination of hands and nails.

Four-stage clearance certification procedure
8.33   Entry into enclosures for four-stage clearance certification carries the potential for asbestos exposure and contamination of clothing. Enclosures have not yet been shown to be asbestos free. Indeed in many cases remedial action is required before clearance is obtained. In addition, dust raising activities will be performed and the analyst may also have to crawl, kneel and climb, causing potential scuffing or tearing of clothes as well as contamination. Therefore analysts should not wear domestic clothing under coveralls. Analysts should wear overshoes or wellingtons or similar. Gloves may also be worn. Where full decontamination is likely to be necessary (see paragraph 9.2), two pairs of disposable coveralls should be worn. The first pair of coveralls can be removed in the airlock and disposed of as asbestos waste on exiting from the enclosure. The second pair can be used to transit between the airlock and the hygiene facility.

Entry into 'live' enclosures
8.34   Analysts should be dressed in appropriate clothing for entry into enclosures where elevated asbestos levels are likely and full decontamination procedures will be necessary. The RPE and PPE will consist of full facepiece powered respirators with P3 filters, disposable undergarments, disposable coveralls (including transiting coveralls if required), and wellingtons or other similar laceless cleanable footwear. Gloves may also be worn.

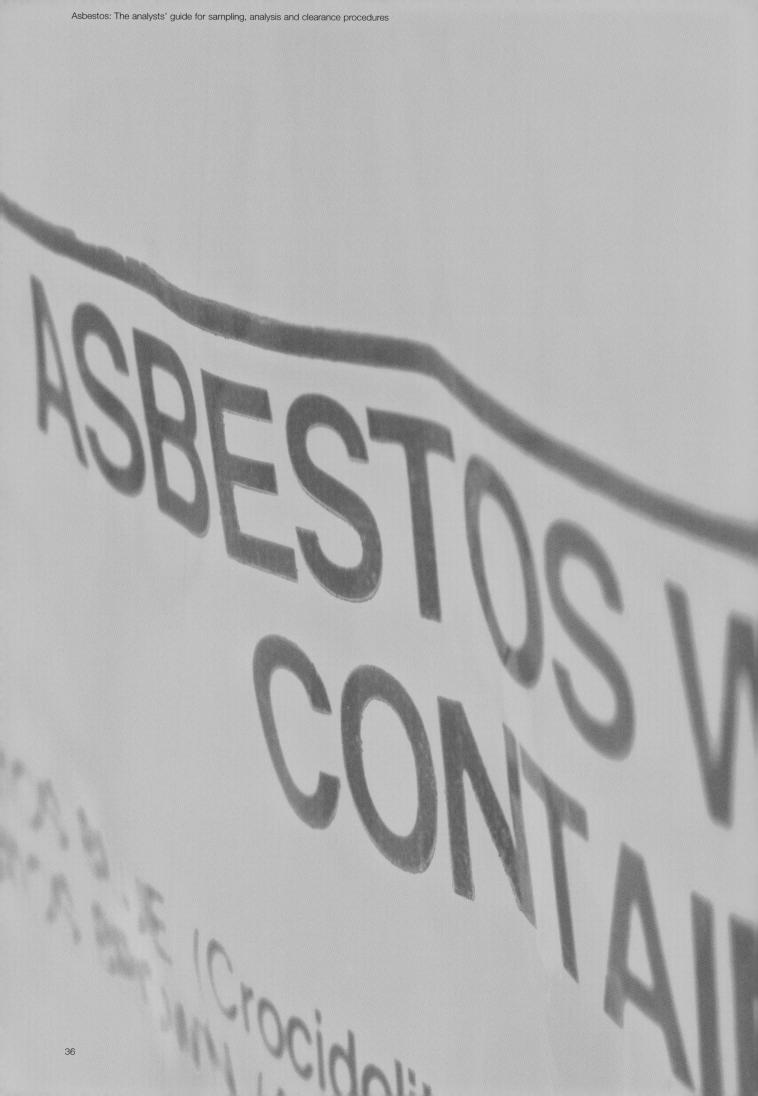

9 Decontamination procedures

9.1   All analysts who enter enclosures or designated work areas may become contaminated with asbestos and therefore need to decontaminate themselves. The purpose of decontamination is to ensure that PPE and RPE as well as the person are cleaned to prevent further spread of contamination. Decontamination must also be performed in such a manner that it does not lead to secondary exposure for the analyst.

9.2   Analysts will need to be properly trained to decontaminate themselves. Analysts who enter enclosures will therefore need to complete practical training as detailed in module 24 of HSG247 *Asbestos: The licensed contractors' guide.*[3] This sets out the full procedures for decontamination. However, in practice, analysts may not need to complete the full decontamination procedure in all cases. Decontamination for analysts can be divided into two categories:

- 'preliminary' decontamination, where little contamination has occurred and which involves the cleaning, removal and disposal of PPE; and
- 'full' decontamination, where significant contamination is possible. This procedure includes preliminary decontamination and further decontamination in a hygiene unit.

9.3   Analysts should always undertake decontamination. The type of decontamination will depend on the activity undertaken and the potential or extent of contamination that occurs during the activity. The required decontamination level should be considered as part of the risk assessment for the work. In many cases, it will be sufficient for analysts carrying out routine site work (eg certification for reoccupation and building surveys) to undertake the 'preliminary' decontamination procedure. However, if analysts are entering enclosures when asbestos removal work is taking place, eg as part of SLH duties, or in the professional opinion of the analyst, there is potential for contamination to occur, (eg crawling through undercrofts to inspect, survey or collect sampling pumps), the analyst should undergo full decontamination on exit from the enclosure. The analyst should therefore dress appropriately for this type of decontamination. In addition there may be circumstances where full decontamination was not planned but becomes necessary.

Preliminary decontamination

9.4   The analyst will need to have available a number of items to allow preliminary decontamination to take place. These include:

- asbestos waste bags: for contaminated PPE, equipment and cleaning materials;
- duct tape: to seal bags;
- wet wipes: to clean respirator, equipment and footwear of surface deposits;
- wet rags, bucket and sponge: if more extensive cleaning is necessary on site.

9.5   For decontamination following entry inside enclosures for Stage 2 and Stage 3 of the four-stage certificate of reoccupation, the analyst should follow the normal decontamination procedures required for exiting this environment. Although removal work is complete, the enclosure is still active and will have a type H vacuum cleaner in place along with buckets of water, brushes and sponges or wipes. These will be located at the edge of the enclosure or in the inner stage of the 3-stage airlock system. The vacuum cleaner should be used to clean RPE and PPE including footwear. The RPE should then be wiped or dampened down using a wet sponge or wipe. Footwear should be cleaned in the bucket using the brush. Sampling equipment should be wiped down in the inner stage. Coveralls should be removed in the middle stage of the airlock and placed in a waste bag. The analyst should exit the airlock system and remove the RPE and place in a waste bag.

9.6   For building surveys, decontamination of footwear is likely to be the most frequent activity. This will be necessary in areas where there is asbestos dust and debris on the floor. If disposable overshoes are worn these can be taken off, bagged and replaced with new ones. Otherwise it may be necessary to wipe down the soles with wet wipes to avoid the spread of asbestos-containing dust and debris. In general the coverall and respirator should be removed on completion of the survey (or at a break) in a safe area, eg in the open air.

Full decontamination

9.7   Full decontamination requires the use of a hygiene facility. This is one of the first items to arrive on a removal site and should be the last item to leave site on completion of the job. The hygiene unit should be available for the analyst to use should it be necessary. Figure 9.1 shows the layout of a typical hygiene facility.

9.8   There are two different forms of the full decontamination process:

- where the hygiene facility is connected via an intervening space or tunnel to the enclosure;
- the use of transit facilities where the hygiene facility is physically separated from the enclosure.

Hygiene facility connected to enclosure

9.9   This form of decontamination process is outlined in Figures 9.2 and 9.3. Hygiene facilities should, where practicable, be positioned close to the work area with an intervening space or tunnel and a one-stage air lock constructed of polythene sheeting, connecting the hygiene facility with the stripping enclosure. See Figure 9.4. The intervening space or tunnel will need to act as an air gap between the enclosure and the hygiene facility and should be provided with a vent to the open air. This method of linking up the hygiene facility to the enclosure should be normal practice unless it is impracticable (eg due to limited space, restricted access and multi-storey work), to site the hygiene facility close to the work area.

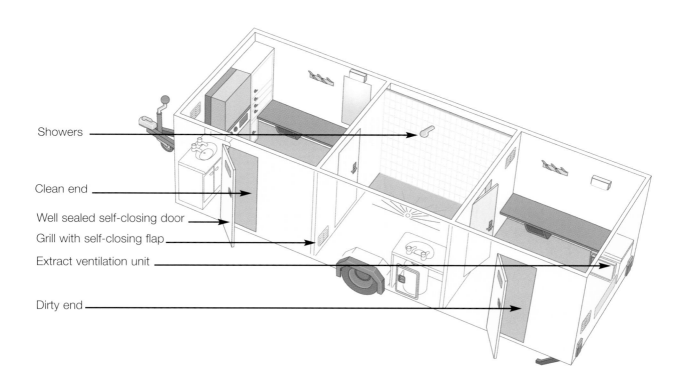

Showers

Clean end

Well sealed self-closing door

Grill with self-closing flap

Extract ventilation unit

Dirty end

Figure 9.1 General layout of hygiene facilities

Figure 9.2 Decontamination process hygiene unit attached to enclosure: Entering enclosure

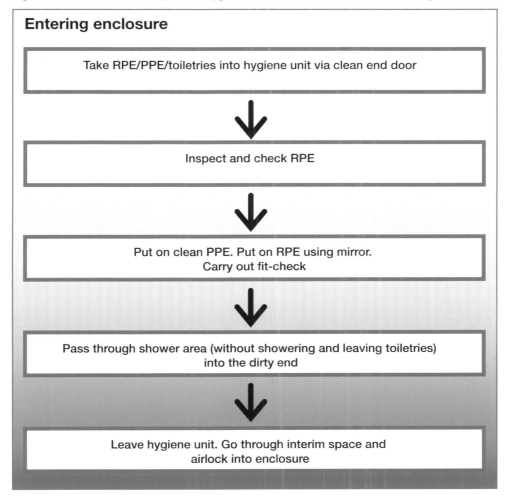

Figure 9.3 Decontamination process hygiene unit attached to enclosure: Leaving enclosure

Leaving enclosure

Leave enclosure and enter airlock

↓

Vacuum all visible dust and fibres from PPE, RPE and footwear. Brush footwear in footbath. Sponge or wipe RPE

↓

Enter dirty end of hygiene unit. Take off all footwear, coveralls and underwear worn in the enclosure and place in storage or disposal bags. Do not remove RPE

↓

Move to shower area with respirator on. Shower and use a sponge to clean RPE without allowing water onto filter ports

↓

Once RPE has been cleaned, remove it and shower yourself thoroughly. Remove used filters and place in waste bag for disposal

↓

Start drying off. Place towel in bag for disposal or laundering

↓

Pass through into clean end and complete drying with a different towel(s). Dress

↓

Leave hygiene facility via clean end external door

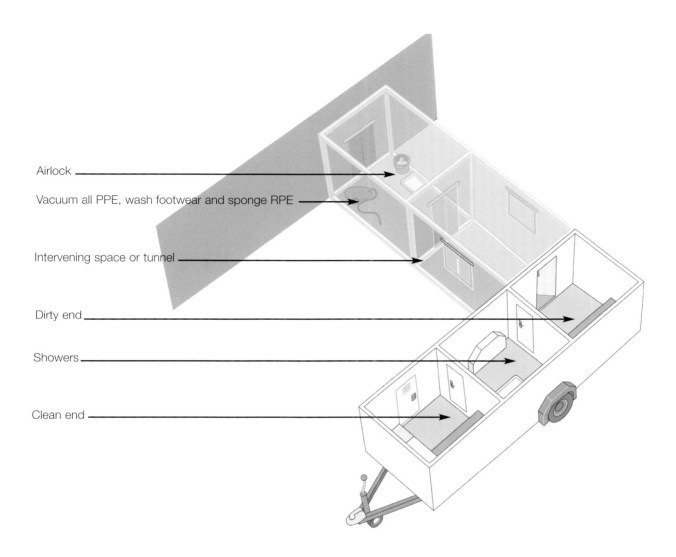

Airlock

Vacuum all PPE, wash footwear and sponge RPE

Intervening space or tunnel

Dirty end

Showers

Clean end

Figure 9.4 Hygiene facility connected directly to the enclosure

9.10   Where it is not possible to connect a hygiene facility directly to the work area then transit facilities will have to be provided to enable workers and analysts to carry out preliminary decontamination before travelling to the main hygiene facility for full decontamination. The process is described in Figures 9.5 and 9.6.

9.11   Transit facilities consist of a three-stage airlock system. The system is attached to the stripping enclosure and comprises three compartments separated by weighted sheets to minimise the spread of dust between the compartments. As seen in Figure 9.7 the inner stage is the compartment nearest to the enclosure, the middle stage is the middle compartment and the outer stage is the final compartment before exiting to walk to the hygiene facility. The minimum dimensions for each compartment are 1 m x 1 m x 2 m. Where space is unrestricted, these compartments should be larger. The three stages should have the following facilities within them:

■   Outer stage: Facilities to store transit coveralls and footwear; eg hooks and/or shoe-holders.
■   Middle stage: Facilities to store coveralls and footwear

worn in the enclosure eg hooks and/or shoe-holders and a waste bag.
■   Inner stage: Vacuum cleaner; footbath and brush; water bucket and sponge or wipes for RPE. (Note that the vacuum cleaner may be located at the edge of the enclosure.)

9.12   The object of the procedure, shown in Figure 9.5, is to remove as much of the asbestos fibre and/or debris acquired in the enclosure as possible. To minimise spread while on the transit route, people should put on transit footwear and a set of transit coveralls, in place of their enclosure coveralls and footwear.

9.13   All transit routes should be delineated to ensure that other workers or members of the public keep away from this route, where practicable. Any contamination found on the transit route at Stage 1 of the four-stage site clearance procedure will delay the provision of a certificate of reoccupation to the client.

9.14   Once the analyst has reached the main hygiene facility, they should decontaminate as normal (see Figure 9.6).

Figure 9.5 Decontamination process transiting procedure: Entering enclosure

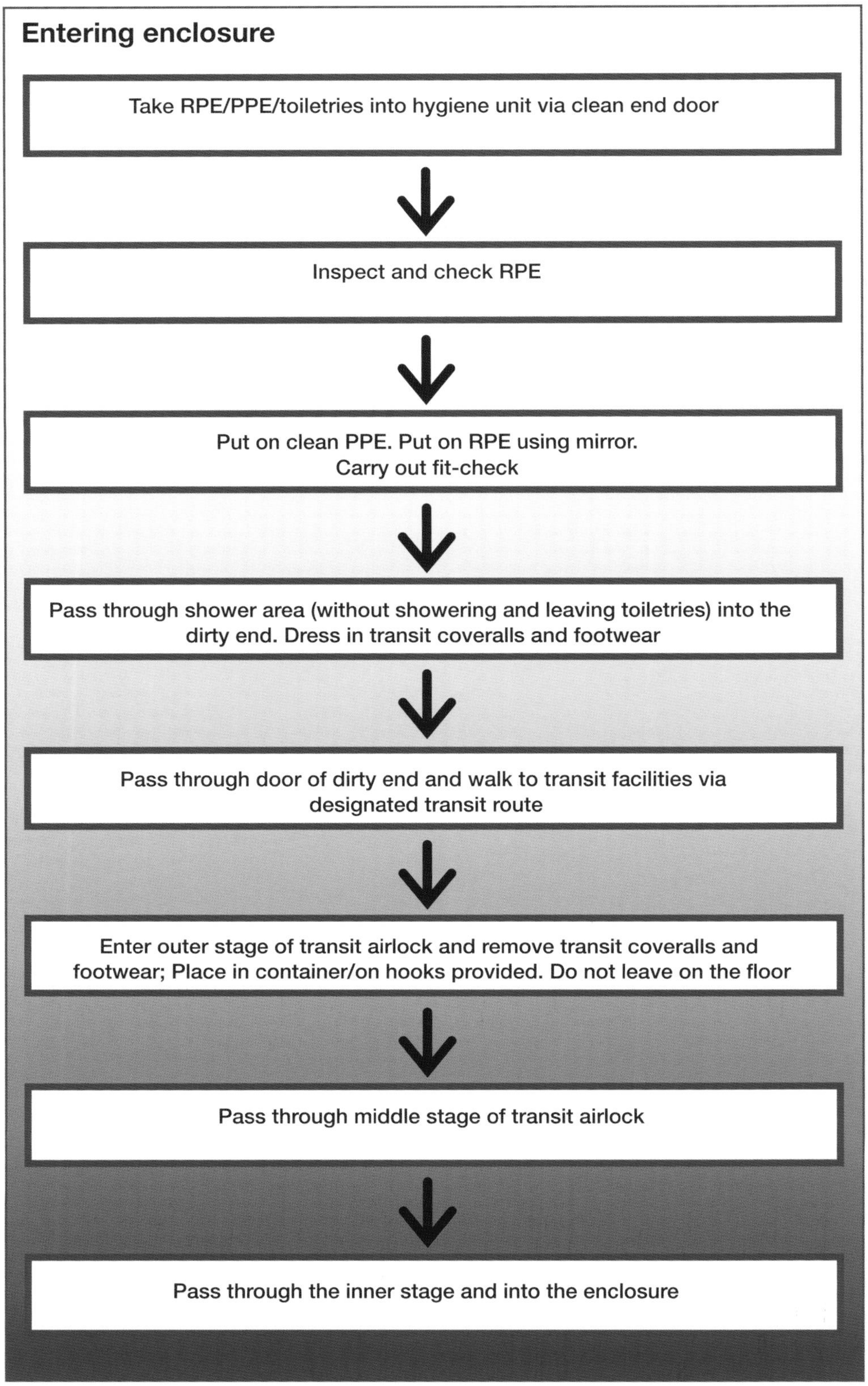

Entering enclosure

Take RPE/PPE/toiletries into hygiene unit via clean end door

$\downarrow$

Inspect and check RPE

$\downarrow$

Put on clean PPE. Put on RPE using mirror.
Carry out fit-check

$\downarrow$

Pass through shower area (without showering and leaving toiletries) into the
dirty end. Dress in transit coveralls and footwear

$\downarrow$

Pass through door of dirty end and walk to transit facilities via
designated transit route

$\downarrow$

Enter outer stage of transit airlock and remove transit coveralls and
footwear; Place in container/on hooks provided. Do not leave on the floor

$\downarrow$

Pass through middle stage of transit airlock

$\downarrow$

Pass through the inner stage and into the enclosure

Figure 9.6 Decontamination process transiting procedure: Leaving enclosure

Leaving enclosure

Leave enclosure and go into inner stage of transit airlock. Vacuum visible dust and fibres from PPE/RPE and footwear. Brush footwear in footbath. Sponge down or wipe RPE

Pass into middle stage of airlock. Remove coveralls and footwear worn in enclosure and place in waste bag (or store if re-entry required). Do not remove RPE

Pass into outer stage. Put on transit overalls and transit footwear. Walk to hygiene facility via designated transit route

Enter dirty end of hygiene facility. Take off all footwear, PPE and underwear worn in the enclosure and place in storage or disposal bags. Do not remove RPE

Move to shower area with respirator on. Shower and use a sponge to clean RPE

Once RPE has been cleaned, remove it and shower yourself thoroughly. Remove used filters and place in waste bag

Start drying off. Place towel in bag for disposal or laundering

Pass through into clean end and complete drying with different towel(s). Dress

Leave hygiene facility via clean end external door

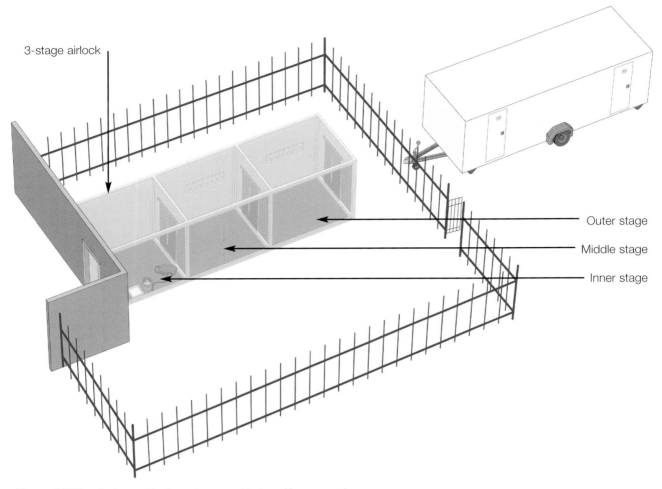

3-stage airlock

Outer stage

Middle stage

Inner stage

Figure 9.7 The 3-stage airlock system used in transiting procedures

9.15   Further details on the construction and siting of hygiene facilities can be found in *Asbestos: The licensed contractors' guide*.[3]

9.16   Equipment taken into the enclosure will normally be clean and can be taken in through the clean end of the hygiene unit or picked up on the transit route. When leaving the enclosure with equipment or sample containers they should be treated as contaminated unless the analyst has decontaminated them first. For the outside of smooth surfaces (eg plastic bags, sample tins, plastic containers) wiping with wet wipes in the middle airlock is sufficient to remove any attached fibres and the decontaminated items can be placed in an appropriately labelled bag or container and removed from the end enclosure. Equipment (eg sampling pumps, rotameters, mirrors, tripods etc) can also normally be wet wiped and placed in a clean polythene bag for removal from the enclosure. Further decontamination may take place on return to the laboratory using appropriate facilities.

Appendix 1: Fibres in air: Sampling and evaluation of by phase contrast microscopy

Important note: This method will supersede MDHS39/4[5] when the UK implements the new EU asbestos workers' directive 2003/18/EC in 2006 and should be used for training and conversion QA-counting only until the implementation date.

Introduction

Nomenclature, appearance and regulation

A1.1   Asbestos is a term used for the fibrous forms of some naturally occurring silicate minerals that have been exploited commercially for their useful properties of flexibility, high tensile strength, incombustibility, low thermal conductivity and resistance to chemical attack. In Britain, the Control of Asbestos at Work Regulations (CAWR)[10] defines and regulates asbestos as the fibrous forms of the following minerals (or any mixture containing them): chrysotile, amosite, crocidolite, fibrous actinolite, fibrous tremolite and fibrous anthophyllite. A population of airborne asbestos fibres, when viewed under a microscope, will often appear to contain many thin parallel-sided fibres and may also contain bundles of parallel fibres, split fibres, curved or wavy fibres and even matted masses. For regulatory purposes, a countable fibre is defined as any object, which is longer than 5 µm, with average width less than 3 µm and having an aspect (length/width) ratio greater than 3:1.

Outline of the method and changes from the previous MDHS

A1.2   The following method is described for the measurement of airborne fibre concentrations, and is due to replace the previously recommended guidance in MDHS39/4.[5] Amendments to the EU directive are due to replace the European Reference Method, (Annex 1 of the original directive 83/477/EEC)[27] with the World Health Organisation (WHO) method[6] for the determination of airborne fibre number concentrations. The WHO method applies to all fibre types and is similar to MDHS59,[28] although in this guidance the method is used specifically to evaluate airborne concentrations of predominantly asbestos fibres. If a mixed fibre population is suspected after the original count is completed, discriminatory counting may take place, using one or more of the techniques outlined in MDHS87.[29]

A1.3   The number of changes from the previous MDHS39/4[5] to comply with the WHO method has been minimised. However, the incorporation of the MDHS into an HSG guidance document has meant that the sampling and analytical strategy and interpretation for sampling other than for compliance monitoring has been included as chapters in the main HSG. This leaves this appendix focused on compliance sampling, analysis and the reporting of the results. This is close to the scope of the WHO method. The major changes introduced by the WHO method are as follows:

- flow rates of up to 16 litres.min[-1] may be used for short-term 10 minute sampling;
- samples should be rejected if the flow rate has varied more than ±10% between flow checks;
- the entire filter should be scanned at low magnification to determine whether the loading is uniform and that there is no gross aggregation of fibres or dust;
- fibres attached to >3 µm width particles are also counted;
- the average fibre width is used to decide whether it is less than or greater than 3 µm;
- fields lying within 4 mm of the filter edge (or 2 µm of a cutting line) should not be counted;
- discrimination between fibre types is allowed after an original non-discriminatory fibre count has been completed (see MDHS87);[29]
- subtraction of the blank count from the fibre count is allowed (but this has not been adopted).

Principle

A1.4   A sample is collected by drawing a measured volume of air through a membrane filter by means of a sampling pump. The filter (or part of the filter) is mounted on a microscope slide and rendered transparent ('cleared'). Fibres of appropriate dimensions on a measured area of filter are counted visually using phase contrast microscopy (PCM) and the number concentration of fibres in the air calculated.

Scope and limitations

A1.5   The method measures the airborne concentration of countable fibres using PCM. Countable fibres are defined as particles with length >5 μm, width <3 μm and aspect ratio (length: width ratio) >3:1. Fibres having widths <0.2 μm may not be visible using this method,[30] and the PCM count represents only a proportion of the total number of fibres present. Therefore the count is only an index of the numerical concentration of fibres and not an absolute measure of the number of fibres present. As part of the UKAS accreditation requirement, laboratories will need to produce their own documented in-house method for air sampling.

Fibre discrimination

A1.6   The method does not identify the fibre type present but fibres with widths greater than about 1 μm may show optical properties that are inconsistent with asbestos and it is permissible to eliminate these fibres from the count to determine compliance with the asbestos control limit or other limits. Alternatively, other methods (eg analytical electron microscopy) can be used to determine the asbestos fibre concentration. **Discrimination against non-asbestos fibres should only take place after the initial total count** has been completed. Any discrimination will be dependent on the range of analytical techniques available, the skills of the microscopist and the strategy used. A hierarchy of methods is available to eliminate non-asbestos fibres such as machine-made mineral fibres (MMMF), vegetable, aramid and other fibre types. A more detailed discussion of these techniques appears in MDHS87.[29] The report of the discrimination evaluation should include a statement on the type and numbers of interfering fibres which were present and the method by which the number of non-countable fibres have been eliminated from the original PCM count. To carry out fibre discrimination, the laboratory will need to be accredited for the discrimination method, as well as PCM fibre counting.

Limit of detection and limit of quantification

A1.7   Particles sampled onto a filter at best have a random distribution. This means that the precision of the count is limited by the underlying 'Poisson' statistics. The precision is usually expressed in terms of the confidence interval, which defines the upper and lower limits expected for a defined percentage of repeat counts. For example 95% confidence limits mean that on average 19 of the 20 values from repeat counts would be within the upper and lower limits. For low counts the lower confidence limit is 0, so a one-sided upper 95% confidence interval is used. For a count of 0 it is 95% probable that the count is <3 fibres.

A1.8   The RICE quality control program has shown that blank filter counts by PCM are low. Of the 40 blank filter samples included in the RICE inter-laboratory counting comparisons,[31] 39 had reference counts ranging from 0.3 f/mm² to 2.5 f/mm². Only 7 of the 2204 results (0.32%), had concentrations outside the acceptable limits (performance band B). These results were obtained from counts of 200 fields and showed that on average <1 fibre per 100 fields was counted. This gives an upper 95% confidence limit that <5 fibres will be counted in 100 fields and similarly <6.5 fibres in 200 fields. This relates to the 'blank' count in paragraph 28, so that it can be argued that 5 fibres per 100 graticule areas should be regarded as the lowest reliably detectable count above background (limit of detection). For a sample volume of 240 litres and 100 fields counted this corresponds to a calculated result of about 0.01 f/ml in the air. A sample volume of 480 litres with 200 fields counted corresponds to a calculated result of 0.003 f/ml. A further analysis of the raw data (after the removal of outliers) was also carried out using two methods. The standard method for defining the limit of detection (LOD) and limit of quantification (LOQ) is based on 3 and 10 standard deviations (5.28 and 17.6 fibres, respectively). The second method uses the underlying definitions on which the above are based, where the LOD is the 99th percentile from 0 and the LOQ is determined within a +30% accuracy (7.6 and 25.3 fibres, respectively). The results from the above analyses of the blank data are therefore consistent with the aim to count at least 20 fibres in 200 fields when measuring low concentrations and, for consistency and uniformity of reporting, this should be used to calculate the limit of quantification.

Reagents

A1.9   Acetone and glycerol triacetate ('triacetin') are required for filter clearance. Analytical grade reagents are not essential, but they must be clean and free from fibres. Excessive water in the acetone may reduce filter clarity. The triacetin should be free from moisture and with no evidence of hydrolysis (possibly indicated by a smell of acetic acid) or other contamination.

Apparatus

Sampling equipment

A1.10   To comply with the WHO standard method, an open-faced filter holder fitted with an electrically conducting cylindrical cowl and exposing a circular area of filter at least 20 mm in diameter, should be used for sampling. Normally the cowl should extend 1.5-3.0 times the effective filter diameter in front of the filter. Several manufacturers produce injection moulded conductive plastic sampling heads, which are pre-loaded with a suitable filter (eg Figure A1.1). Alternatively, metal cowls with a PTFE O-ring can be

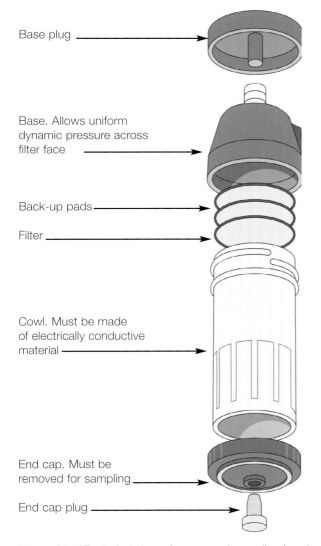

Base plug

Base. Allows uniform dynamic pressure across filter face

Back-up pads

Filter

Cowl. Must be made of electrically conductive material

End cap. Must be removed for sampling

End cap plug

Figure A1.1 Exploded view of a personal sampling head

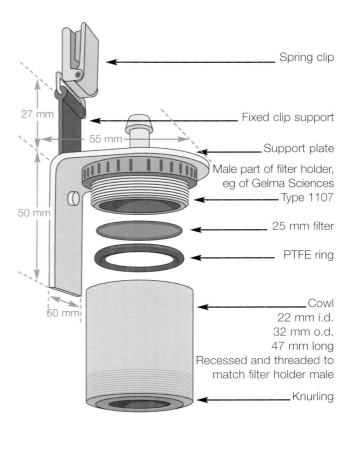

Spring clip

Fixed clip support

Support plate

Male part of filter holder, eg of Gelma Sciences Type 1107

25 mm filter

PTFE ring

Cowl
22 mm i.d.
32 mm o.d.
47 mm long
Recessed and threaded to match filter holder male

Knurling

27 mm

55 mm

50 mm

50 mm

Figure A1.2 Exploded view of a personal sampling head with a metal cowl

purchased (Figure A1.2). A cowled filter holder is intended to protect the filter, while still permitting a uniform deposit. The cowl is pointed downwards during sampling. Flexible tubing is required to connect the filter holder to the pump, and a cap or bung is needed for the cowl entrance to protect the filter from contamination during transport. Different filter diameters and shorter cowls can be used if they are shown to give comparable results, but must be measured to determine the effective filter area.

A1.11 The exposed area of filter must be known and the diameter of the exposed area should be measured to the nearest millimetre (mm) (ie within ±5%) for each type of cowl or O-ring in use. A suitable method of measuring this is to use the filter holder and cowl to sample from a cloud of dark coloured dust. The filter is mounted on a slide in the usual way and the diameter measured using the microscope stage vernier by traversing at low magnification across the diameter of the dark area. Alternatively the diameter can be measured with vernier callipers. At least two diameters should be measured at right angles, and a minimum of three filters from similar holders or O-rings should be checked in

this way. (Differences between these six measurements of more than one millimetre may indicate either a poorly fitting filter holder or an unsatisfactory clearing technique.) An uneven appearance at one edge of the deposit or signs of dust outside the exposed areas indicates that there was a leak in the sampling head.

A1.12 The membrane filters must be of mixed esters of cellulose or cellulose nitrate, of pore size 0.8 to 1.2 μm (optically clear grade). Preferably the filter should be 25 mm in diameter with a printed grid. Take care to avoid contamination when handling filters. Printed grids are on the sampling side of the filter and will be in the same plane as the particles collected and therefore provide a useful focussing aid. Any distortion of grid lines indicates poor mounting procedure.

A1.13 The pump must be capable of:

■ giving a smooth airflow;
■ having flow set to within ±10% for flow rates ≤ 2 litres.min^{-1} and within ±5% for flow rates >2 litres.min^{-1};
■ maintaining this flow rate during the period of sampling.

These values include any change of flow rate with pump orientation. For personal sampling the pump must be light and portable, and capable of being fitted to a belt or carried in a pocket. The pump's battery must have sufficient power to operate within the specified flow limits for the duration of the measurement. If pumps for static samples are operated by mains electricity, give due regard to appropriate safety precautions. Static sampling pumps should have the facility to enable the sampling head to be positioned between 1-2 m above ground level.

Flow measurement

A1.14 The airflow must be measured by a working flow meter, sufficiently sensitive to be capable of measuring the appropriate flow rate to within the values specified in paragraph A1.13, and which has been calibrated against a primary standard. The flow meter incorporated in the pump may only be used if it meets the requirements above and it has been calibrated against a primary standard or a master flow meter with a loaded filter in line. Float type flow meters should be vertical when read. Under normal operating conditions, the measurement of temperature and pressure is not necessary, as it will only make a small difference to the total uncertainty, eg if the field temperature changes by +30°C from the calibration temperature, the correction is ~5%, which will contribute to only a small increase (0.2%) in the maximum calculated uncertainty, due to systematic errors (see Table A1.2). Pressure difference of +40 millibars from the calibration pressure will give a correction of ~2%. Only at high pressure and low temperatures, eg +40 millibars and -20°C from the calibration conditions will the readings be underestimating by more than 5%. Normally, rotameter markings are set for standard temperature and pressure (293°K and 101.3 kP (1013 mbar) and any laboratory calibration will be carried out in similar conditions. Only in exceptional circumstances and if a float type flow meter (rotameter) is used will there be a need to use the following equation to adjust the flow rate read from the calibrated rotameter:

$$Qa = Qc\sqrt{\frac{Pc.Ta}{Pa.Tc}}$$

Where: Qa = sampling flow rate in litres.min^{-1}
Qc = calibrated flow rate the rotameter value in litres.min^{-1}
Pa = air pressure at sampling site in kPa
Pc = air pressure at site of calibration in kPa
Ta = air temperature at sampling site in °K
Tc = air temperature at site of calibration in °K

(Note: the standard metrological unit for reporting atmospheric pressure is hectopascals (hP) where 1 hP = 0.1 kP = 1 millibar.)

A1.15 The length of the flow meter tube, the range of airflow covered and the spacing and number of markings will directly affect the accuracy of reading and the calibration. To a large extent, the accuracy of the reading of the external

flow meter is part of the pump performance assessment in paragraph A1.13, if it is used to check the flow rate. The airflow and hence the float, must be sufficiently stable in the flow meter tube to enable a precise reading against the tube markings. From a practical point of view to set the flow rate to ±10% at 0.5 litres.min^{-1} (the minimum recommended value) a minimum tube distance of 10 mm for each 1 litres.min^{-1} division is required. This means that the pump flow must be sufficiently stable and adjustable so the float must be able to be positioned and read to within ±0.5 mm of the 0.5 litres.min^{-1} flow mark. Longer distances between the markings and the markings at higher flow rates, will give proportional increase in the accuracy of reading. A float type flow meter tube must be marked with an appropriate number and scale of markings to allow the flow rate to be set, within the limits defined in paragraph A1.13. If a master flow meter is used to calibrate the field flow meter, the laboratory will need to demonstrate that the two flow meters can be read and used to give sufficient accuracy, so that airflows can be set to within the ranges specified in paragraph A1.13. This is usually achieved by having larger spacing between the airflow markings than the minimum values given above.

A1.16 Bubble flow meters measure the volume of air displaced by the pump directly and have advantages in that they do not need correction for changes in air pressure and temperature and their accuracy of flow measurement is much better than a float type flowmeter, if used within the specified range of airflows. It is important to ensure that there are no leaks or significant additional constrictions in the sampling train between the sampling head and the flow meter and that the inlet of the flow meter is to atmosphere. Otherwise, any flow meter will potentially give an erroneous value.

A1.17 The primary standard or master flow meter should preferably be a flow meter whose accuracy is traceable to national standards. These should only be used for in-house calibration of the working flow meters and should be used with careful attention to the conditions of the calibration certificate. The recalibration of the master and working flow meters should be related to the amount and type of use and any evidence that is available to show their stability over time. Procedures are given in the WHO method[6] for in-house calibration against a bubble flow meter, although many prefer to send their master flow meters for recalibration to an accredited calibration laboratory.

Equipment for filter clearance

A1.18 Filter clearing should be accomplished by the acetone/triacetin hot block method (Figure A1.3). A syringe is normally required to dispense the acetone and fine-tipped pipettes, or other suitable droppers, are needed to dispense triacetin.

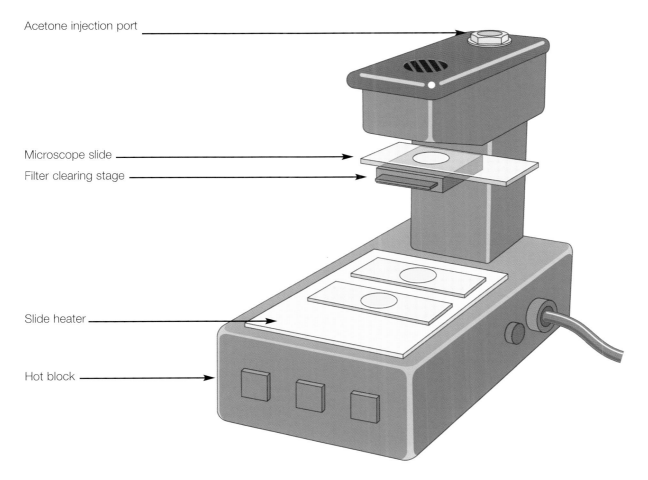

Acetone injection port

Microscope slide

Filter clearing stage

Slide heater

Hot block

Figure A1.3 Example of a hot block for clearing filters

Microscopy

A1.19 The visibility of fine fibres by PCM is dependent on the transparency of the mounted filter, the quality and cleanliness of the microscope's optics, its correct use and maintenance, the operator's eyesight and other factors. Differences between the smallest fibre width observable by phase contrast microscopes will contribute to differences between counters (because fibre width distributions extend below the detection limit). To maintain a uniform level of detection at the limit of visibility, the microscope and accessories should comply with the following specifications:

■ a binocular stand with Köhler, or Köhler type illumination including a field iris. (The condenser (sub-stage assembly), objectives and eyepieces specified below must all be compatible with each other and with this stand.);

■ a sub-stage assembly, incorporating an Abbe or an achromatic phase contrast, condenser in a centrable focusing mount, with phase annulus centring independent of the condenser centring mechanism;

■ a built-in mechanical stage with slide clamps and x-y displacement;

■ a low powered objective (eg X 10 or X 4 magnification), which is used for carrying out checks on the evenness of the dust deposit on the filter and locating the stage micrometer and test slide 'tramlines';

■ a positive phase contrast objective (preferably par focal with the low-powered objective) of magnification X 40; the numerical aperture (NA) of this objective (which determines resolving power) must lie between 0.65 and 0.70; the phase ring absorption must lie between 65% and 85%;

■ an optically matched pair of binocular eyepieces, preferably of the wide field, high eye-point type, providing a total magnification of at least X 500 (one of the eyepieces must be of the focusing type and must permit insertion of a graticule);
(Note: Some microscope stands may include a tube extension, which increases the total magnification. The total magnification is calculated by multiplying the objective, tube extension and eyepiece magnifications together. This total should not exceed 1000 times the NA);

■ a Walton-Beckett eyepiece graticule,[32] type G22, with an apparent diameter in the object plane of 100 ±2 μm (when checked against a calibrated stage micrometer) must be used to define the counting area;

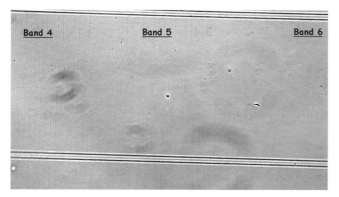

Figure A1.4 View of visible blocks on a HSE mark II/mark III test slide

- various accessories including:
  - a phase telescope or Bertrand lens to ensure correct alignment of the phase rings;
  - a green filter (optional) which assists viewing (as the optics are optimised for green light);
  - a calibrated stage micrometer of 2 μm divisions (eg type S12);
  - an HSE mark II or mark III test slide (see Figure A1.4 and paragraph A1.32).

A1.20 The coverslip and slide will also affect the visibility of fine fibres. Both must be of glass and of appropriate thickness. Microscope slides must be of conventional type: eg approximately 76 mm x 25 mm and preferably 0.8 mm to 1.0 mm thick. The coverslip thickness is specified/marked on the objective (eg 0.17) and the appropriate thickness must be used (usually sold as 0.16 to 0.19 mm thick, eg No. 1½) and should be about 25 mm diameter or about 25 mm². The microscope slides and coverslips should be clean and conform to relevant standards.[33]

Sampling

Preparation of filter holders

A1.21 If a filter holder and cowl is being reused it must be cleaned. Filters should be loaded, unloaded and analysed in an area as free from fibre contamination as practicable. Care must be taken to handle the filter at all times with clean flat-tipped tweezers and only gripping the filter at the edge, outside the exposed area. The printed grid on the filter should be placed in the filter holder, so that it faces towards the cowl. The entrance to the cowl should be closed with a protective cap or bung when sampling is not in progress. Push-fit cowls, particularly if they are reloaded, are prone to poor sealing and should always be checked for tightness. To improve the tightness of the seal, push the cowl entry down very firmly onto a hard surface with a slight rocking action (with the protective entry cap removed). Additional shrink seal bands to reduce the likelihood of leakage from push-fit cowls can be applied to the outside of the seal after loading. Screw-tightening cowls should always be checked for tightness before use: overtightening will damage the filter and cause leakage through the filter, insufficient tightening would allow leakage around the edge of the filter.

Sampling period, flow rate and volume

A1.22 The sampling procedures and strategy should be designed where possible to give sample densities within the range for optimum accuracy (100-650 f/mm²) or to ensure that the minimum limit of quantification is based on at least 20 fibres. The recommended flow rates and sampling times for various sampling strategies are given in the main guidance.

Pump preparation

A1.23 Pumps with poor flow control may change their flow rate during the initial warm-up period. To stabilise the flow rate, some pumps may need to be run for 10-15 minutes before resetting the flow rate, unless there is evidence (eg sampling data and/or manufacturer's instructions) to show that this is unnecessary with the type of pump in use. A separate filter and filter-holder should be dedicated to this, and may be used for several pumps before being discarded. Pumps should be capable of maintaining flow for the intended sampling period (eg up to 4 hours). Particular care should be taken with short period samples because flow instability at the start may have a significant effect on the apparent volume collected.

Sampling

A1.24 For personal sampling, the filter holder should point downwards and be fixed to the worker's clothing (eg upper lapel, hood or shoulder), as close to the mouth and nose as practicable, and preferably within 200 mm. Due regard must be given to localised concentrations: in such cases, the sampling head should be positioned on the side expected to give the higher result. If a respirator is worn, the sampling head should be positioned away from the clean exhaust air. Static samples are taken using a downward pointing filter holder positioned some 1-2 m above floor level and away from any walls or large obstructions. Each filter holder should be uniquely identified and the person or position it is used to sample recorded, along with the date and other relevant site information (eg the type of activity taking place and any environmental factors that may affect the results).

Taking the sample

Time and flow-rate recording
A1.25 At the start of the sampling period, the protective cap must be removed from the filter holder, the pump started and the time noted. The flow rate should be measured and recorded at the start and the end of the sampling period. At the end of the sampling period the time should be recorded, the pump stopped and the protective cap replaced on the filter holder. The sampling period must be measured to within ±2.5%. The average flow should be calculated. Periodic checking and adjustment of the flow rate can be made and this should be recorded and used in the final calculations of the average flow. The flow variation between the start and the end of the sampling period should be maintained within ±10% or the sample rejected.

Filter handling and transportation
A1.26 The preferred procedure is for the filter to be transported in the capped filter holder, but if for some reason

this is not possible, the filter may be removed in a clean area and carefully placed (with exposed face upwards) in a clean tin or similar container with a close-fitting lid. The filter should be handled with tweezers, which are used to grip the unexposed edges. **Sprays (eg cytology fixative) must not be used to 'fix' the dust to the filter.** If a tin or container is used for transport, unless it can be guaranteed that it will be carefully handled and remain upright, adhesive tape should be used to secure the clean unexposed edge of the filter to the container. The filter can be cut free for mounting and analysis using a surgical scalpel with a rolling action. **Care must be taken not to contaminate the filter at any stage or to dislodge any deposit.** The filter holder and cowl or the container must be thoroughly cleaned and dried before reuse.

Blanks

A1.27 There are three types of blanks.

■ **Sampling media blanks** are generated when filters are extracted from a box of unused filters. They are mounted and counted before sampling to check that the batch of filters is satisfactory; the initial procedure is to select at least 4 blank filters from each manufacturers' batch (or a minimum of 1% from larger batches) before the filters are used. Individual blank filter counts should not normally exceed 3 fibres per mm^2 (2½ fibres per 100 fields) and if laboratory records show that the proportion is consistently higher, the causes (including the source of supply) should be investigated.
■ **Field blanks** are generated when filters are taken from satisfactory batches to the sampling area and subjected to the same treatment as filters used for sampling, (the cap is removed and replaced after a few seconds). The filters in capped, cowled heads are taken to the sampling area without having air drawn through them and without them being attached to the worker (the cap is removed and replaced after a few seconds). A field blank should normally be nominated for each job and sent with the field samples to the laboratory.
■ **Laboratory blanks** are generated when filters, extracted from satisfactory filter batches, are mounted and counted to check for laboratory contamination, if a field blank has indicated a need for investigation. A laboratory blank may be evaluated with each batch of routine samples, or afterwards, if contamination due to laboratory sources is suspected.

A1.28 The type and number of blanks that are available for analysis and are analysed, will depend on a number of factors. Sampling media blanks are analysed before sampling to check they are suitable for use. The sampling agency is responsible for initiating field blanks and the laboratory will normally know from the sampling information supplied that they are included. The laboratory should always ensure that at least one field or one laboratory blank is prepared for each batch or group of samples, so that it can, if necessary, check whether the source of any fibre contamination was due to the filter preparation. Normally, if low counts are obtained from some of the field samples it will not be necessary to analyse the field or laboratory blanks. If elevated counts are obtained on all the field

samples, at least one field blank (or if not available, one laboratory blank) must be counted for each batch to exclude the possibility of contamination. Laboratories should investigate the source of any blank contamination and monitor the batch-to-batch consistency of membrane filters. Due to the low numbers of background fibres present, **blank counts must not be subtracted from sample counts.**

(Note: the WHO method calls for subtraction of the blank count, but this guidance has not adopted this procedure except as an additional stage, if contamination on the blanks has been found. Evidence shows that the blank count should normally be low and will make little difference to compliance measurements.)

Filter clearing and mounting

A1.29 If additional analytical work to discriminate between fibre types is required (see MDHS87)[29] then samples and blank filters may be cut in half with a scalpel using a rolling action, with the filter carefully held at the edge. Half of the filter can then be mounted, and the other half suitably stored and kept for subsequent investigation if necessary. All samples must be uniquely labelled.

A1.30 **The acetone-triacetin mounting method must be used**. The principle is that condensing acetone vapour collapses the filter pores, adhering the filter to the glass slide and turning it into a transparent plastic film with any asbestos fibres contained close to the upper surface. Triacetin is used to provide the interface between the collapsed filter and the coverslip. The mounted slide will keep for years without noticeable deterioration, although small-scale fibre movement may occur. Slides should be stored carefully and not subjected to extremes of temperature. They should be preserved with all relevant records for at least six months so that the result can be checked if necessary.

A1.31 The filter to be mounted is placed centrally on a clean microscope slide, sample side upwards, and preferably with grid lines parallel to the slide edges. It is important that the filter is free from excessive moisture as water interferes with the clearing process. If samples have been exposed to high humidity, it may be necessary to dry the filters before mounting. This can be done by placing the filters and containers in a warm air cabinet (without a fan), or slide warmer before mounting, making sure the lid of the container is at least partly removed to allow water vapour to escape. A ring of metal or inert plastic placed around the filter helps to localise the spread of acetone and improves the efficiency of clearing. The minimum volume of acetone to completely clear the filter should be used (~0.25 ml). The slide (which must be clean) is placed under the outlet orifice of the hot block (see Figure A1.3). The acetone is injected slowly into the hot block so that the vapour emerges in a steady stream over the filter. The filter should clear instantly. This small amount of acetone minimises fire and health risks. However, all sources of ignition should be remote, and the acetone storage bottle should be stoppered when acetone is not being extracted. **Acetone vapour is highly flammable and slightly toxic and the appropriate safety precautions should be taken before this procedure is** used. (The procedure may be conducted in a fume-cupboard to minimise inhalation of acetone vapour.) The slide may be placed on a hot plate at 50-60°C for a few seconds to evaporate any excess acetone before applying triacetin and the coverslip. When the acetone has evaporated, a micropipette or other suitable dropper is used to place a drop or two of triacetin on the filter (~120 μl). This must be just enough to cover the filter when the coverslip is in place, without overflow around the edges. The clean coverslip is lowered gently at an angle onto the filter so that all the air is expelled. It should not be pressed onto the filter, or moved, once it has been lowered into place. If necessary any excess triacetin can be carefully removed from the slide using a corner of a tissue, or similar, to absorb the excess fluid by capillary action. The coverslip should not be touched or wiped in any way. At this stage the filter will still appear grainy under the microscope. If counting is to take place immediately, it should be placed on the hot plate (eg for up to 15 minutes at 50-60°C) to produce a more transparent mount. If left overnight at room temperature, the filter will 'clear' without any heating. The slide should be kept clean in a horizontal position (coverslip side up), until it is cleared and counted.

Evaluation

A1.32 The microscope must be adjusted and used according to the manufacturer's instructions, and the analyst must check its performance at the beginning of each counting session (or more frequently if any adjustments have been made). A typical sequence for checking that the microscope is correctly adjusted is:

- place, centre and focus the working stage micrometer, preferably using bright-field illumination. If necessary use the low-powered objective to help locate the 0-100 μm scale, then return to the X 40 objective;
- adjust field iris and condenser height to obtain Köhler or Köhler type illumination;
- check (and adjust if necessary) that the inter-ocular distance is correct for the user, the image has sharp focus in both oculars and that the Walton-Beckett graticule is also in sharp focus;
- measure and record the diameter of the Walton-Beckett graticule against the stage micrometer (it should be in the range of 98-102 μm). **The measured diameter must be used in calculations;**
- remove the stage micrometer and replace with the HSE mark II/mark III test slide;
- centre and focus the test slide using phase contrast microscopy, (if necessary use dark field illumination and a low-powered objective to help locate the two sets of parallel grooves (tramlines) in which the test grating is located, before inserting the X 40 phase objective);
- check using a Bertrand lens or phase telescope that the phase rings are concentric and centred: adjust if necessary;
- check and readjust the field iris and condenser height at the working magnification to obtain Köhler or Köhler type illumination;
- record which of the seven bands is just visible (lines only partly seen) by traversing from the most visible to the least visible;
- the ridges of block 5 of an HSE mark II test slide must

be visible, while only parts of block 6 ridges may be visible and none of block 7 ridges should be visible at the working magnification (see Figure A1.4). Mark III test slides issued with a red certificate require that block 4 must be visible while only parts of the block 5 ridges may be visible and none of the block 6 ridges should be visible;
- the focus and condenser focus will need readjustment before each filter is counted.

Other sequences can be used provided all the necessary adjustments and checks are made.

A1.33 The slide with the mounted filter is placed on the microscope stage. The sample should be examined with a low power objective to check the uniformity of the deposit and that there is no gross aggregation of fibres or dust on the mounted filter. The filter should be discarded if badly non-uniform or overloaded with particles so that it is difficult to count. Fibres on the filter must be counted using at least X 500 magnification (Note: if higher magnifications are used they should not exceed 1000 times the numerical aperture of the objective lens). The fine focus must be adjusted upwards and downwards by several micrometers at each new area to ensure that all fibres are seen. The counting should proceed according to the following rules:

- graticule areas for counting must be chosen at random to avoid bias and to be representative of the exposed filter area. Fields lying within 4 mm of the filter edge (or 2 mm of a cutting line) should not be counted. Fields should be rejected if:
  - a filter grid line obstructs all or part of the field of view;
  - more than one eighth of the graticule field area is occupied by an agglomerate of fibre and/or particles, by discrete particles or by air bubbles;
  - the microscopist judges that fibres are so obscured that they cannot be counted reliably.

If the number of rejected fields exceeds 10% of the number accepted, or the microscopist judges the sample to be uncountable or biased, this should be noted in the final report.

- a countable fibre is defined as any object which is longer than 5 μm, with an average width less than 3 μm and having an aspect (length/width) ratio greater than 3:1 (fibres attached to particles are assessed as if the particle does not exist and are counted if the visible part of the fibre meets the above definition);
- The following recording rules apply:
  - a countable fibre with both ends within the graticule area is recorded as one fibre;
  - a countable fibre with only one end in the graticule area is recorded as half a fibre;
  - a countable fibre passing through the graticule area, and having no ends within that area, is not counted;
- a split fibre is taken to be one countable fibre if it meets the definition above, otherwise it should be ignored; a split fibre is defined as an agglomerate of fibres which at one or more points on its length appears to be solid and

undivided, but at other points appears to divide into separate strands; the width is measured across the undivided part, not across the split part;

■ loose agglomerates of fibres are counted individually if they can be distinguished sufficiently to determine that they meet the definition above;

■ fibres in a bundle and tight agglomerates of fibres, where no individual fibres meeting the definition of a countable fibre can be distinguished, are taken to be one countable fibre if the bundle or agglomerate as a whole meets the definition above;

■ if the width of the fibre varies along its length, a representative average width should be considered.

Examples depicting countable and non-countable fibres, and which display one or more of the features described above, are given in Figures A1.6a-f.

A1.34 The number of graticule areas counted depends on the sampling situation as follows:

■ for evaluations related to personal sampling in connection with compliance sampling and the assessment of respirator protection, **at least 100 fibres must be counted or 100 graticule areas must be inspected,** whichever is reached first; at least 20 graticule areas must be inspected even if these contain more than 100 fibres;

■ for evaluation of other samples (eg clearance indicator, background, reassurance and leak sampling), **200 graticule areas must be inspected on samples of the minimum of 480 litre volume.** If the collected air volume (v) is more than 480 litres, the number (n) of graticule areas inspected may be reduced proportionately according to the formula n = 96 000/V. For example, if 960 litres is collected, only one hundred graticule areas need be examined. It may not be necessary to examine n graticule areas if a clear decision can be reached at an earlier stage: for example, if 30 fibres in 200 fields would give a calculated concentration of 0.015 f/ml, then it may be possible to report an enclosure as unsatisfactory as soon as a count of 30 fibres is reached (even if only a few graticule areas have been examined). Where 2 or more samples are being pooled to obtain 480 litres (or a larger volume), V is the total volume of the pooled samples and **n is the same number of graticule areas inspected on each of the pooled filters.**

Figure A1.5 Examples of fibre counting rules for single fibres

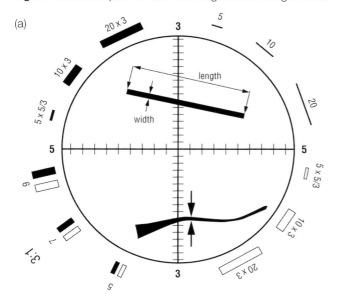

(a)

1 fibre; meets length, width and aspect ratio criteria

1 fibre; the width being measured at the 'average' point

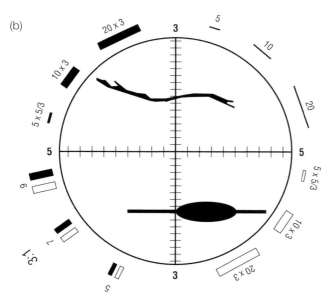

(b)

1 fibre

1 fibre; ignore the particle or 'bulb' of resin when estimating the width

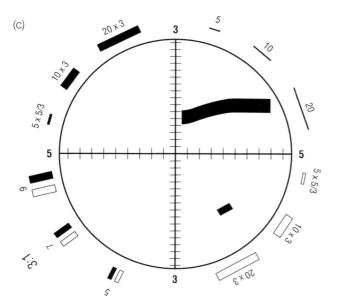

(c)

0 fibres; width too large

0 fibres; aspect ratio is less than 3:1

Figure A1.5 Examples of fibre counting rules: for fibres within graticule area and split fibres

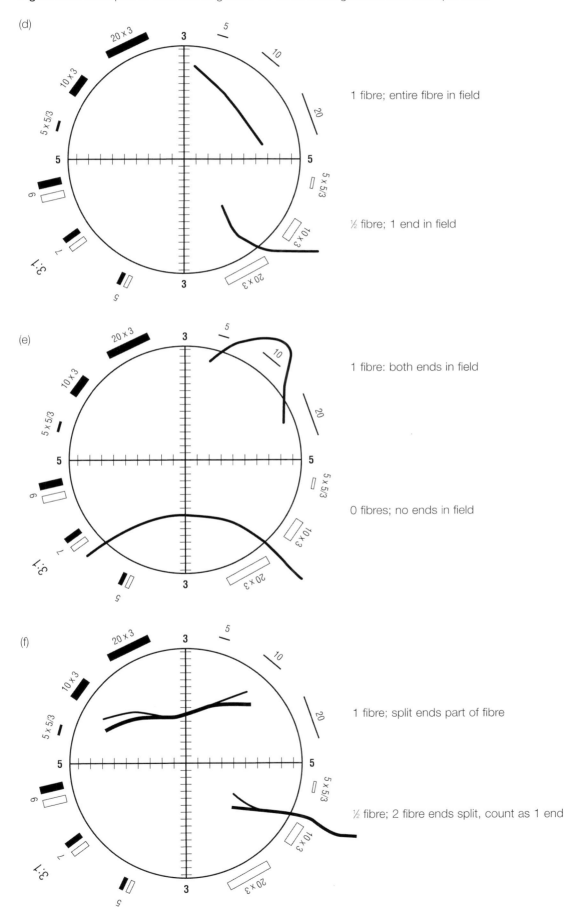

(d)

1 fibre; entire fibre in field

½ fibre; 1 end in field

(e)

1 fibre: both ends in field

0 fibres; no ends in field

(f)

1 fibre; split ends part of fibre

½ fibre; 2 fibre ends split, count as 1 end

Figure A1.5 Example of fibre counting rules for grouped fibres

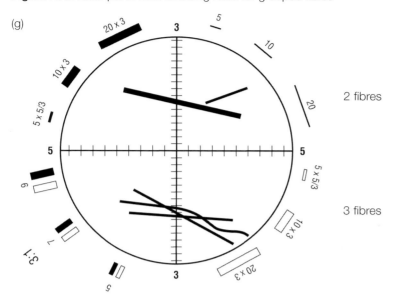

(g)

2 fibres

3 fibres

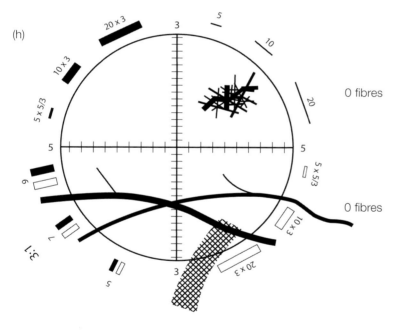

(h)

0 fibres

0 fibres

Figure A1.5 Example of fibre counting rules for fibres in contact with other particles

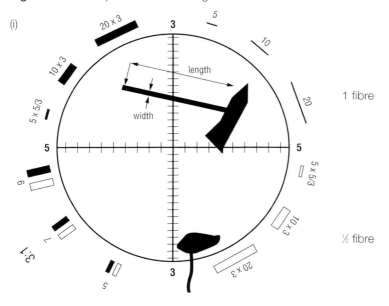

(i)

1 fibre

½ fibre

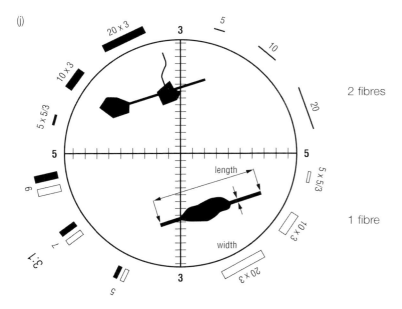

(j)

2 fibres

1 fibre

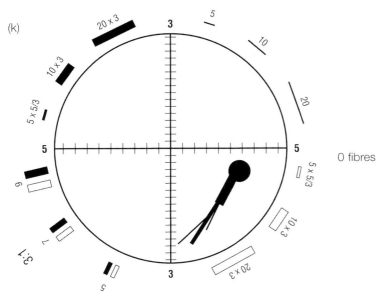

(k)

0 fibres

Figure A1.5 Example of fibre counting rules for fibres in contact with other particles

(l)

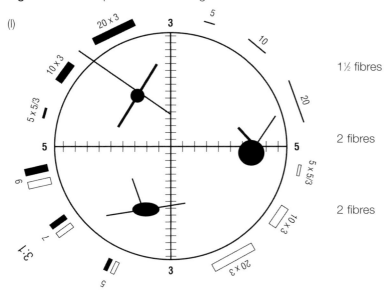

1½ fibres

2 fibres

2 fibres

(m)

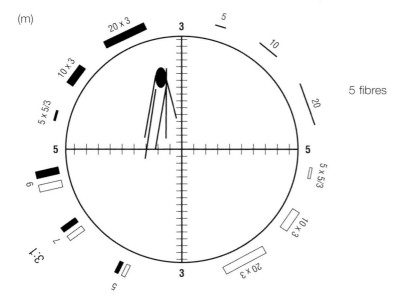

5 fibres

Calculation of results

A1.35 The airborne concentration is given by the formula:

$$C = 1000 \, N \, D^2 / V \, n \, d^2 \text{ fibres per millilitre (f/ml)}$$

where N is the number of fibres counted;

 n is the number of graticule areas examined;
 D (mm) is the diameter of the exposed filter area;
 d (μm) is the diameter of the Walton-Beckett graticule;
 V (litres) is the volume of air sampled through the filter.

When pooling 2 or more samples, V is the total volume sampled, N is the total number of fibres and **n is the number of graticule areas examined on each filter** (which is the same for each filter and not the total number examined). The concentration result must be calculated correct to sufficient decimal places to determine whether it is above or below the specified limit (eg for 0.2 f/ml calculate to 2 decimal places, for 0.01 f/ml calculate to 3 decimal places).

A1.36 The following points should be noted in relation to measurements.

■ Sampling for comparison with control limits may be carried out for a set time or for the duration of a specific activity. Ideally, a time-weighted average should be calculated based on a continuous 4-hour sampling period. However, in many circumstances (eg asbestos removal and maintenance work), continuous 4-hour or 8-hour sampling is not possible, as the duration of the work is too short and activity-related sampling is carried out). A time-weighted average for a fixed time period can be calculated if additional sampling of other activities (eg tea and lunch breaks) are included or an assumption that no exposure is taking place is made.
■ Even when continuous sampling is possible, high particulate concentrations may require that shorter sampling periods are used to yield countable filters and samples must be pooled together, to calculate a time-weighted average.

Recording and reporting results

A1.37 All relevant sampling and analytical information should be recorded. The sampling records should include relevant site information and contain sufficient information: to establish the traceability of any calibrations, to calculate the results and to assure the quality of the sampling. The analytical records should contain sufficient information: to establish the traceability of the calibrations, to calculate the results reported and to assure the quality of the analysis. The report should include sufficient information on the sampling and analysis so the results are traceable and the purpose and outcome of the sampling are clear. Normally, results are also covered by a laboratory's UKAS accreditation (see CAWR 2002)[10] and additional information (see Lab 30)[20] may be required to be recorded and reported. As sampling and analysis may be carried out by different individuals and bodies, the analytical report should either append or contain the appropriate sampling

information. All test reports should conform to ISO/IEC/17025 requirements.[20]

A1.38 Any report should include the following information:

■ the name or letterhead of the body carrying out the work;
■ the full postal address of the body and other electronic contacts;
■ the UKAS accreditation mark and number (and any appropriate disclaimer);
■ the printed name(s) of the person(s) who carried out the work;
■ the printed name and signature of the person who authorised the release of the report (this may be the same person who carried out the work);
■ the date the report was authorised for release;
■ a suitable report identifier or number.

The sampling report should also include:

■ the location of the sampling (eg name and address);
■ the date of sampling;
■ the type of sampling being carried out;
■ the sampling information for each sample, including:
  - a unique identifier (eg sample number);
  - the type of sample (eg personal or static and compliance, background, clearance etc);
  - the position of the sample: (eg the name of the or location);
  - the sampling time started and ended for each period;
  - the calculated volume of air sampled;
  - reference to any specific activities or events taking place during the sampling (eg during demolition, immediately after demolition etc).

The analytical report should also include:

■ the method of analysis used and for each sample;
■ the sample number;
■ the volume of each sample (if not given elsewhere);
■ the fibre concentration;
■ the limit of quantification.

(The reported concentration should not imply greater accuracy than can be justified by the limit of quantification, eg a 480 litre volume sample with 200 fields counted will be reported as <0.01 f/ml or rounded to two decimal places if >0.01 f/ml.)

A1.39 As well as containing the information reported, the sampling and analysis records may also include:

■ the sampling strategy, including any variations from standard procedures (eg for very dusty conditions, sampling times may need to be very short to prevent overloading and a stopwatch may give a more accurate measure of the sampling period);
■ any relevant environmental conditions which may significantly influence the results (eg fog or rainfall if sampling outside, large temperature and pressure differences between the calibration and field conditions for float type flow meters);

- the type of filters in use and batch number;
- the type and identifier for the flow measurement device;
- the type and identifier for the air sampling pump;
- the identifier for the timing device;
- the measured flow rate at the start and end of each sampling period and any checks in between;
- the name of the analyst(s) carrying out the fibre counting;
- the identifier for the stage micrometer;
- the identifier for the test slide;
- the measured diameter for the Walton-Beckett graticule;
- the block number where the gratings are still visible on the HSE test slide;
- number of graticule areas examined for each sample;
- number of fibres counted for each sample;
- the measured diameter and calculated area of exposed filter;
- the upper and lower 95% confidence limits of the fibre count;
- the overall uncertainty; and
- any additional information for the discrimination counting (see MDHS87)[29] strategy.

Human factors

A1.40 Take care to ensure that the ergonomic and working practices and the working environment in a laboratory have no adverse influence on the accuracy of the counts. There should be sufficient legroom and clearance so that adjustable seating can be adjusted to allow the microscopist to sit in a well-supported, relaxed and comfortable manner. To avoid eye fatigue, the light intensity of the microscope and surroundings should be comfortable to view. Also, the ambient light should not be brighter than the microscope and should not reflect off the coverslip or optics or cause any other source of glare. Any peripheral view beyond the microscope should be, if possible, an unobstructed distant view in unchanging light. Alternatively, a matt background shield can be used. Poor posture may lead to neck and back strain and poor lighting or incorrect microscope adjustment will lead to eyestrain, all of which will adversely influence counts produced by the microscopist. Adjustments of the inter-ocular distance and for the different focal lengths of each eye are quick but important and should be carried out by the microscopist at the beginning of each counting session. The eyes should not be too close to the oculars and if high eye point wide-field binoculars are used those not wearing glasses should make use of the eye shields. The microscope image should be sufficiently vibration-free that particles in the field of view are both steady and clear.

A1.41 Limits must be placed on the amount of fibre counting undertaken by analysts in specified periods because fatigue can adversely affect the quality of counts. The number of graticule areas examined in any 8-hour period by one counter should not normally exceed 2400, the equivalent of 12 samples if 200 graticule areas are examined on each. Counters are recommended to take a break at least after every third or fourth slide counted in succession, and if long shifts are worked, additional quality assurance (QA) measures may be necessary. The length and frequency of the fibre counting sessions will depend on the

microscopist, the type of samples and the laboratory conditions. The number of samples evaluated in a day also differs from microscopist to microscopist: typically, counters may take 10-25 minutes to evaluate a sample with a sparse dust deposit, but longer for greater numbers of fields and more difficult samples.

Accuracy

A1.42 It is not possible to know the 'true' airborne fibre concentration of a given dust cloud and the absolute accuracy of the method cannot be assessed. However, some information is available about relative bias associated with sample evaluation. Microscopists generally undercount dense deposits. When sampling fibres in atmospheres relatively free from interfering particulates, the density range for optimum accuracy should be in the range 100-650 fibres/mm^2;[34] for densities above 650 fibres/mm^2 the results may be underestimates (but no attempt should be made to correct them) and above 1000 fibres/mm^2, fibre levels are subject to increased undercounting and are normally too dense to count. In mixed dust situations, the presence of other fibres and particles may interfere with the accuracy of results. Chance superimposition of non-fibrous particles may cause fibres not to be counted fully, by a proportion, which depends on the mean size and concentration of the non-fibrous particles but not on the fibre concentration.[35] In practice, the effects of chance superimposition on counts are small compared with subjective effects and will not be important for the counting rules defined in this method. An important factor is that the counting procedure can result in systematic differences in counts produced by different microscopists within and, more particularly, between laboratories. These intra- and inter-laboratory differences must be controlled by proper training and periodic quality checks.

Precision

A1.43 Counting precision depends on the number of fibres counted and on the uniformity of the fibre distribution on the filter. The latter may be described reasonably by the Poisson distribution. Theoretically the process of counting randomly distributed (Poisson) fibres gives a coefficient of variation (CV) = $1/N^{1/2}$, where N is the number of fibres counted. Therefore the CV is 0.1 for 100 fibres and 0.32 for 10 fibres counted. In practice, however, the actual CV is greater than these theoretical numbers due to an additional component associated with subjective differences between repetitive counts by one microscopist and between replicate counts by different microcopists: this CV is given approximately by the formula $(N + 0.04N^2)^{1/2}/N$, where N is the mean number of fibres per evaluation;[36] typical CV values are given in Table A1.1 and Figure A1.7 for intra-laboratory counts. If n fibres are found in a single evaluation, the mean of many repeated determinations on equal areas is expected to lie within the confidence limits M95 and M05 on 90% of occasions[36] where:

$$0.91 \, M_{95}^2 - (2n + 2.25)M_{95} + n^2 = 0,$$

$$0.84 \, M_{05}^2 - (2n + 4)M_{05} + n^2 = 0.$$

These equations have been used to calculate the upper and lower confidence limits shown in Table A1.1. It can be seen from this that counting more than 100 fibres gives only a small increase in precision. Also, the method loses precision as fewer fibres are counted; this loss of precision increases as counts drop below about 10 fibres. Inter-laboratory CVs can be twice the intra-laboratory coefficients, or even greater if quality control is poor.

Table A1.1 Intra-laboratory coefficient of variation (CV) associated with number of fibres counted

Number of fibres	Expected CV	Expected 95% confidence limits for the mean of repeated determinations	
		Lower	Upper
5	0.49	1.64	13.01
7	0.43	2.66	16.38
10	0.37	4.81	21.32
20	0.3	10.34	37.41
50	0.25	29.66	84.77
100	0.22	62.59	163.16
200	0.21	128.87	319.67

Uncertainty budget

A1.44 The UKAS Lab 30 document,[20] which gives guidance on ISO/IEC 17025,[37] requires that the variation associated with each part of the measurement is used to calculate the overall uncertainty (also referred to in UKAS documents as total uncertainty and expanded uncertainty). Various levels of complexity[38, 39] are recommended, but the overall uncertainty for air monitoring of fibres is a function of the systematic, subjective and random errors associated with the air sampling and fibre counting. It is normal practice to represent the overall uncertainty in terms of the 95% confidence interval (this is equivalent to the standard uncertainty times, a coverage factor of 2 for a normal distribution). In a first approximation, the uncertainty due to the systematic errors associated with the analysis are small, when compared to the random errors due to the placement of the sampler and the random distribution of fibres on the filter. As fibre counting is carried out manually, there is also a substantial subjective error that will vary with a whole range of factors for the same counter and between counters. Due to the large random and subjective variability associated with manual fibre counting and that the underlying random Poisson distribution is not symmetrical, the overall uncertainty can only be derived from repeated blind measurements of the same sample. The results from observations from within (intra-) laboratory counts

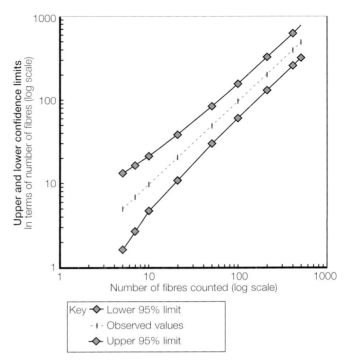

Figure A1.6 Graph of the calculated intra-laboratory confidence limits

are given in Table A1.1 and Figure A1.6. The uncertainty from between (inter-) laboratory counts is best represented by the RICE performance limits.

A1.45 Examples of the factors that contribute to the systematic variability within a laboratory are given in Table A1.2. Both the maximum allowed variability as defined in the method and the typical values measured are evaluated. In some cases a maximum variation has not been specified in the method and a value of 1% has been adopted. In practice,[38] if the variation is <20% of the largest variable, it is usually regarded as negligible. It can be seen from Table A1.1 that the 95% confidence interval from fibre counting, for a count of 20 fibres is between 48 and 187%. The systematic uncertainty from sampling and calibration is calculated (Table A1.2) and combined with the fibre counting variables (Table A1.3) using the root sum square method that treats all the variables as independent. As the maximum allowed systematic uncertainty in Table A1.2 is between ±26% of the mean count, this gives a calculated 95% confidence limit for the overall uncertainty of between 55-191% of the average value. The more likely value of the systematic error calculated in Table A1.2 is ~11%. Even assuming the systematic error is the maximum allowed the overall effect of the systematic errors is less than 20% of the fibre counting error for counts of up to 200 fibres (see last two columns of Table A1.3). This means all the systematic errors from calibrations, timing and flow measurement could be regarded as negligible, compared to the random and subjective errors from fibre counting and the 95% confidence limits derived from the equations in paragraph A1.41 and Table A1.1, and these adequately describe the overall uncertainty.

Table A1.2 Example of an uncertainty budget for systematic variables

Variable	Maximum allowed variability ±%	Example of the measured variability
Sampling variables		
Master flow meter calibration	1	0.5
Working flow meter calibration	3	1.9
Pump flow rate calibration	3	1.9
Pump flow rate variability	10	3*
Rotameter readability (if used)	3	2.5
Time of sampling	2	1*
Sampling uncertainty	11.5	4.9
Analysis variables		
Master stage micrometer	1	0.5
Calibration of sub-master	1	0
Calibration of graticule	2	0
Area of exposed filter	5	2
Analytical uncertainty	5.6	2.1
Overall systematic uncertainty	12.8	5.3
95% confidence interval	±25.6	±10.6

Note: When no figure was available or stated for the maximum allowed variability a value of 1% has been used. Existing calibration measurements have shown that there was no change in the master stage micrometer over the last 17 years and the total uncertainty for calibration of the sub-masters and the graticule over a long period was 0.

Table A1.3 Effect of random and systematic errors

Number of fibres	Maximum allowed systematic errors (±%)	95% confidence limit of fibre counts for random and subjective errors		Total uncertainty for fibre counts as a percentage of the count		Effect of the maximum systematic error as a percentage of the random and subjective errors	
		Lower	Upper	Lower	Upper	Lower	Upper
20	26	10.34	37.41	54.85	190.85	4.18	11.95
50	26	29.66	84.77	48.28	174.24	6.33	15.74
100	26	62.59	163.16	45.56	168.30	7.53	17.88
200	26	128.87	319.67	44.06	165.24	8.28	19.27

Quality control

A1.44 Employers must ensure that the laboratories which they use for the sampling and analysis of airborne asbestos meet the necessary standards set out in ISO/IEC 17025.[37] Employers can satisfy this responsibility by using laboratories that hold UKAS accreditation for asbestos sampling and asbestos fibre counting. UKAS publishes guidance,[20] which discusses accreditation for asbestos sampling and analysis. Laboratories are responsible for ensuring the work is carried out by competent trained staff. The training may include formal training and qualification from organisations participating in the Faculty of Occupational Hygiene within BOHS S301 module for asbestos and other fibres. New staff will need at least a qualification in the BOHS proficiency modules P403 asbestos fibre counting and P404 air sampling and clearance testing of asbestos. Suitable in-house training and performance monitoring of laboratory staff must be carried out to ensure the quality of the results.

A1.45 An essential part of quality assurance is participation in internal and external quality control schemes. This is particularly appropriate for this method because of the large differences in results within and between laboratories obtained with all manual fibre counting methods. Laboratories using this method therefore must participate in the **Regular Interlaboratory Counting Exchanges (RICE)** scheme. This provides a measure of the laboratory's performance in relation to other counting laboratories. Participation in RICE must be supplemented by checks on internal consistency, which should aim to measure and control the individual counter's performance relative to other counters in the laboratory. The internal quality control scheme should incorporate the use of both reference samples (ie those which have a well-defined result established as a mean of a number of determinations), routine samples (ie those which have been analysed in the course of normal work) and blanks. Participation and assessment of individual performance should be carried out at least once a month. Systematic records of quality control results must be maintained and the assessment of performance must be to a defined set of criteria.

A1.46 If it is suspected that the HSE mark II/mark III test slide has deteriorated in quality due to damage or other factors then it should be re-evaluated. HSL should be contacted for advice (see paragraph A1.47).

Advice

A1.47 Advice on this method may be obtained from the Health and Safety Laboratory (HSL) (see 'Further information' for their address). Suggestions for improvement should be sent to the same address.

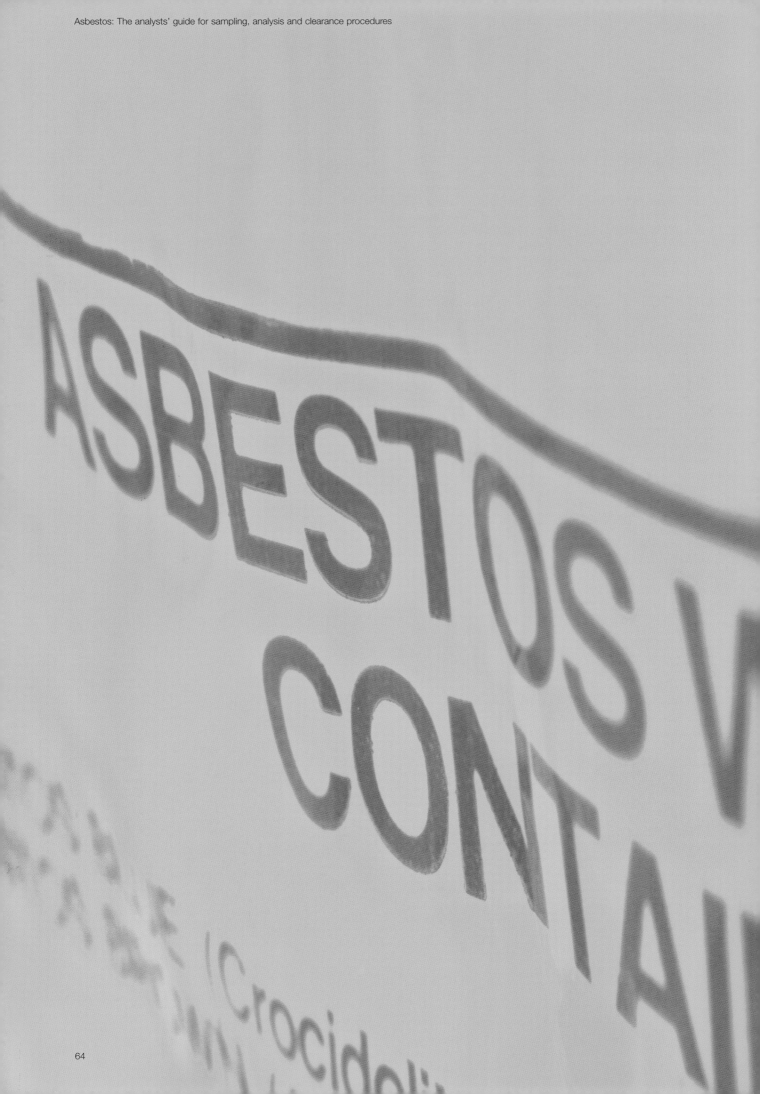

Appendix 2: Asbestos in bulk materials: Sampling and identification by polarised light microscopy (PLM)

Introduction

Definitions and nomenclature

A2.1   Asbestos is a term used for the fibrous forms of several naturally occurring silicate minerals that have been exploited for their useful properties of flexibility, high tensile strength, incombustibility, low thermal conductivity, and resistance to chemical attack. For regulatory purposes in Britain, the Control of Asbestos at Work Regulations (CAWR)[10] define asbestos as any of the minerals chrysotile, crocidolite, amosite, fibrous anthophyllite, fibrous actinolite or fibrous tremolite (see Table A2.1), or any mixture of them. 'Asbestos-containing material' is a term used to describe a material which contains any of these regulated fibrous minerals. The nomenclature and definitions used in this Appendix to describe optical microscope work are based on the RMS Dictionary of Light Microscopy;[40] see the 'Glossary of terms'.

Mineralogy of asbestos

A2.2   Silicate minerals are classified by the number and arrangement of silicate tetrahedra in the repeating units of the crystal lattice.[41, 42] Chrysotile is classified as a sheet silicate and is a member of the serpentine group.[41, 43] The other types of asbestos are chain silicates in the amphibole group of minerals.[42, 43] Rocks containing serpentine and amphiboles occur widely on the earth's surface, but only in rare circumstances have conditions favoured the formation of asbestos, which occurs in veins. When veins are present in significant quantities (above about 1% of the host rock) commercial extraction of the fibres may be practicable. It is not uncommon for relatively low percentages of asbestos to be present in other mined products (such as talc and iron ore). Table A2.1 gives the asbestos and the non-asbestos varieties of the serpentine and the amphibole minerals together with nominal compositions.[43-47] Variations in cation composition not only define the amphibole types, but are also responsible for the observed differences in optical properties within each type. Microscopists should be aware of such variations and their effects on observable refractive indices (RIs); see paragraphs A2.4 and A2.41.

Table A2.1 Varieties of regulated asbestos, their non-asbestiform mineral analogues, and nominal compositions (adapted from Hodgson[44] and Walton[47])

Asbestos variety	Non-asbestos mineral analogue	Nominal composition
Serpentine group of minerals		
Chrysotile	Lizardite, Antigorite	$Mg_3(Si_2O_5)(OH)_4$
Amphibole group of minerals		
Crocidolite	Riebeckite	$Na_2Fe_3^{2+}Fe_2^{3+}(Si_8O_{22})(OH)_2$
Amosite	Grunerite	$(Fe^{2+},Mg)_7 (Si_8O_{22})(OH)_2$
Fibrous anthophyllite	Anthophyllite	$(Mg,Fe^{2+})_7 (Si_8O_{22})(OH)_2$
Fibrous actinolite	Actinolite	$Ca_2(Fe^{2+},Mg)_5 (Si_8O_{22})(OH)_2$
Fibrous tremolite	Tremolite	$Ca_2Mg_5(Si_8O_{22})(OH)_2$

Principle

A2.3   A representative sample of the material thought to contain asbestos is collected for examination. In the analytical laboratory, this is examined by eye, followed by more detailed examination using a low power (X 8 to X 40) stereo-microscope. One or more representative sub-samples may be prepared mechanically and/or chemically for further examination. Fibres observed in the course of these examinations are categorised tentatively on the basis of morphology and certain physical properties. Each fibre type so recognised is sampled by selecting a few fibres or bundles, and these are mounted in a refractive index (RI) liquid chosen to match the most likely asbestos type. The fibres then are positively identified as one of the six regulated asbestos types on the basis of their detailed optical properties using polarised light microscopy (PLM) with magnifications from about X 80 upwards, as appropriate to the type of sample.

Scope and limitations

A2.4   This Appendix describes the identification of the six regulated types of asbestos by PLM (paragraphs A2.7-A2.40). The method is suitable for all common asbestos-containing materials, and can distinguish between asbestos fibres and elongate mineral fragments or other materials in almost all situations. However, difficulties may occur in distinguishing between fine (<1 μm width) fibres, tremolite and actinolite or between tremolite and anthophyllite (see paragraph A2.41) in such cases electron microscopy with energy dispersive X-ray analysis and/or electron diffraction techniques, X-ray diffraction or infra-red spectroscopy may be required to provide additional information. Also, information is given on asbestos that has been subjected to heat[48-50] (see paragraph A2.44) and on other types of fibre which may be encountered[51] (see paragraphs A2.45-A2.54).

A2.5   The sampling procedures to obtain samples of ACMs for analysis can be found described in Chapters 3-4. MDHS100, *Surveying, sampling and assessment of asbestos-containing materials*,[8] describes surveying techniques and bulk sampling strategy and procedures.

Sensitivity

A2.6   With careful application of this method, a single fibre may be found in a few milligrams of dispersed material. In theory, for a fibre about 100 μm long by about 2 μm diameter, this implies a detection limit in the order of 1 ppm by mass. With such a sensitive method **it is important that all procedures be designed to avoid cross-contamination.**

Analysis

Procedure

A2.7   This Appendix describes analytical techniques that have been shown to give reliable and reproducible results.

Alternative methods can be used if equivalence in terms of detection and identification can be demonstrated. Identification of the asbestos fibres should be based on the following analytical sequence (see also Figure A2.1, and the detailed procedures given in paragraphs A2.15-A2.40):

■   a preliminary visual examination of the whole of the bulk sample is made to assess the sample type and the required sample treatment (if any): where possible a representative sub-sample may be taken at this stage;
■   sample treatment is undertaken (if required) to release or isolate fibres;
■   a detailed and thorough search under the stereo microscope is made to classify the fibre types present;
■   representative fibres are mounted in appropriate RI liquids on microscope slides;
■   the different fibrous components are identified using PLM.

If no asbestos is identified by these procedures, additional searches for small asbestos fibres on random sub-samples of a few milligrams are undertaken using PLM (see Figure A2.1 and paragraph A2.23).

Precautions

A2.8   **Handling procedures should be such as to minimise the risk of releasing fibres into the laboratory.** Visual and stereo microscope examinations, and sample preparation, should be conducted inside a fume cupboard, or in a suitable cabinet. Sealed bags or containers of asbestos samples should be opened only inside such a cabinet or fume cupboard. Heavy duty plastic bags are recommended for temporary containment of waste prior to final disposal in properly labelled bags (see 'Asbestos label'). Chemicals used in sample preparation are subject to the Control of Substances Hazardous to Health (COSHH) Regulations 2004,[52] and should be fully assessed prior to use. When the handling of asbestos-containing materials is frequent, airborne exposures should be assessed as required by CAWR.[10] In any case, it is recommended that regular air monitoring (on a monthly basis) is conducted in the preparation/identification area, and that the results are recorded.

Laboratory requirements

A2.9   Fume cabinets should conform to BS 7258,[53, 54] and in practice should have a minimum face velocity of 0.5 m/s. Recirculating air cabinets must draw air away from the microscopist, and be fitted with a high efficiency ('HEPA') filter. Ergonomic laboratory design is recommended for easy movement between areas used for sample preparation and analysis. Adjustable seating to allow the microscopist to sit with a relaxed and comfortable posture is particularly important. A background shield may be required if other sources of light or activity interfere with the microscopists comfort or concentration. Ideally, to avoid eye fatigue, the peripheral view beyond the microscope should be distant and without direct sunlight.

Figure A2.1 Initial examination of samples

Unpack samples in safety cabinet and carry out initial visual or preliminary stereo microscopy observations

Describe sample as homogenous or non-homogeneous (describe each individual layer by colour, texture, and if possible, material type). Take sub-samples if necessary

If necessary, remove interfering matrix materials which may hamper identification

Conduct careful search of the sample under the stereo microscope using the tweezers, and probe to find and isolate fibres

Fibres observed

Note individual fibre types by observing appearance and handling properties under the stereo microscope

Make tentative identification of fibre types present

Extract several fibres or fibre bundles of each type of asbestos and tease apart

Mount in matching RI liquid for PLM identification (see Figure A2.2 for choice of liquid)

Fibres not seen

Consider further sample preparation to see if fibres are still embedded or encapsulated

Take small random samples and place each between two microscope slides and disperse by gentle grinding, then draw apart[+]

Place RI liquid on coverslip and invert onto slide and allow capillary action to immerse sample. Scan the sample at X 80 or greater* for fine fibres using PLM or PCM

If fibres observed prepare additional slides for PLM identification

If no fibres observed report result

+ Note: Hard materials may scratch the slide or be too large to form a satisfactory mount. Dispersing sub-samples in a liquid by shaking and waiting a few seconds for large particles to settle out before pippetting one or more drops onto a microscope slide and drying can also be used.

* Note: Fine chrysotile fibres were commonly used in some commercial products (eg vinyl asbestos floor tiles and decorative/textured coatings). Fine asbestos fibres may also be present in some mineral products and settled dusts. Higher magnifications eg using X 500 phase contrast microscopy (PCM) optics may be used to search for fine asbestos fibres. Increased visibility and contrast can be obtained by using liquids with a large RI difference from the fibre (eg for chrysotile use water, or a liquid of RI = 1.67).

Reagents

A2.10 Various reagents may be necessary for sample treatment. Acetic acid, hydrochloric acid, sodium hydroxide, and acetone or other organic solvents, are commonly used. Liquids of known RI are needed. To identify the six asbestos minerals, a minimum of five high dispersion liquids having RI values 1.550, 1.605, 1.640, 1.670 and 1.700 is used commonly, but other RI liquids may be required to achieve RI match between fibre and liquid (see also paragraph A2.40). The commercially available RI liquids have a stated shelf life. For the reason outlined in paragraph A2.6, contamination by particles and fibres during use should be avoided; therefore, it is recommended that the liquids be checked on a regular basis in the quality control programme, and that suitable records of such checks be kept[20] (see also paragraph A2.57).

Sample preparation and analytical equipment

A2.11 Apparatus required for sample treatment will include probes and needle point tweezers, and also may include glass beakers, disposable containers or washable Petri dishes, an ultrasonic bath, boiling tubes, vacuum filtration flask, pump and filter holder with appropriate filters (glass fibre and cellulose filters are not recommended because they may introduce fibres into the sample). Pliers, a file and a saw may be needed to break the sample, and a pestle and mortar may be needed to release fibres from matrices. For analysis the following equipment is required: glass slides, cover slips,[32] probes, tweezers and lint-free tissues.

Microscopes

A2.12 A low powered stereo microscope is required for the initial search. A polarised light microscope capable of Köhler (or Köhler type) illumination is needed for fibre identification: if it has an in-built light source, the instrument must have an independently centrable condenser; also required are:

- a focusable condenser with numerical aperture (NA) greater than that of any objective used;
- a condenser iris;
- a polariser;
- a removable analyser;
- a removable first order red compensator (of retardation approximately 530 nm);
- a level rotating and independently centrable stage (or a level rotating stage and centrable objective);
- a focusing eyepiece (preferably non-rotatable) containing a cross-hair graticule defining the vibration directions of the polariser and the analyser;
- a Bertrand lens or focusing phase telescope;
- eyepieces of X 8 or higher magnification (those with high eyepoints and flexible caps for spectacle wearers are advantageous);
- objectives of X 10 (minimum NA = 0.2) and higher magnification (higher NA).

Note: In some microscopes filters may reduce the light intensity and should be removed for satisfactory PLM work.

Additional equipment for RI assessment

A2.13 One of the following accessories is required to aid the assessment of fibre RIs by producing intense dispersion staining colours (see also paragraph A2.39):

- either a dispersion staining objective (X 10 magnification) with a central stop in its back focal plane, used in conjunction with the condenser iris (which is capable of producing a pin-hole aperture);[15] or
- positive phase contrast objective (X 10 magnification or greater), and condenser with matching centrable phase annuli.

Reference samples

A2.14 Reference samples of the six asbestos types listed in paragraph A2.1, and commonly occurring non-asbestos fibres, including natural organic fibres (such as cotton and hair), synthetic organic fibres (such as aramid, polyester and rayon), man-made mineral fibres (for example, mineral wool and glass fibre), and naturally occurring mineral 'fibres' (such as wollastonite and diatom fragments), should be held by the laboratory. Asbestos reference samples suitable for polarised light microscope analysis[55] have been prepared under contract to HSE. Contact HSL for further information. Other asbestos reference materials may be useful. It is recommended practice for analytical laboratories to establish their own libraries of in-house standards related to their work (see also paragraph A2.58).

Detailed analytical procedures

Initial examination

A2.15 The entire sample should be examined by eye to describe the type of material or product present, and to establish whether or not visible fibres are present. The natures of any binder materials should be noted, as they may influence treatment of the sample. Examination of insulation samples and many manufactured products under the stereo microscope will aid the detection of fibres and allow some initial assessment of the number of fibre types present. Certain products such as vinyl floor tiles, textured coatings and settled dusts, may contain asbestos fibres that are too fine to be detected in this initial examination. The appearance, colour and texture of the sample, and any fibre types observed, should be recorded. For non-homogeneous samples, each separate layer, part or variant may require individual description. Sample preparation and the analysis of the sample are dependent on the quality of the initial visual examination. Also, adequate description of the appearance of the sample is important in establishing where, or in which part, the asbestos material is present.

Sample treatment

A2.16 The purpose of sample treatment is to release fibres from any matrix and to remove fine particles adhering to the fibres (both of which obscure optical effects and hinder identification). Non-friable samples will need to be broken (with tools if necessary) and the newly fractured edges inspected under the stereo microscope to reveal protruding fibres. Some hard pieces may require grinding. Surfaces and edges may be abraded to release fibres. **Routine procedures for sample treatment used in the laboratory should be fully documented. Any deviations from these procedures for particular samples should be recorded.**

A2.17 Dilute acetic acid (eg 50%) or cold dilute hydrochloric acid (eg 10%) may be used to remove calcium carbonate and calcium silicate, which are common binders in insulation and asbestos boards, and are used as fillers in floor tiles. Sufficient acid should be added in small aliquots for several minutes or until effervescence stops. Fibre release may be aided by stirring or by ultrasonic treatment. The sample is then filtered and repeatedly washed with water. (Residual acid may degrade the fibres and affect the optical properties, and small crystals of salts will form.) The sample may be rinsed with acetone or other volatile solvents to reduce drying time.

A2.18 Organic binders (for example, in plastics, bitumen, resin or rubber products) may require prolonged treatment in solvents. An effective solvent for any single sample can only be established by trial and error. Some organic binders may be removed by ignition at 400°C, but the optical properties of the asbestos fibres may be modified (see paragraph A2.44).

Stereo microscopy

A2.19 The original samples or portions of sample that have undergone sample treatment should be examined using the stereo microscope. For many asbestos samples a low power stereo microscope (X 10) is suitable, but for other samples higher magnifications are sometimes necessary to examine detected fibres. The aim is to detect small fibre bundles, or individual fibres, and to assess the proportion of fibres present and tentatively assign fibre types based on their appearance. This is usually achieved by placing the sample in a suitable container and performing a detailed search of the whole sample using needles or tweezers to separate the different fibrous components from the matrix. These fibres are then observed under the stereo microscope and their appearance noted. The care and vigilance with which the sample is examined at this stage are important in detecting trace quantities of asbestos. Representative fibres or fibre bundles can be selected and mounted for PLM.

A2.20 Layered samples should be described by their appearance and each layer noted as a separate entity. Other types of non-homogeneous samples will require detailed visual examination. A rigid sample (such as a tile) should be broken, and the surfaces and edges scraped. All observations should be recorded.

A2.21 Generally asbestos is recognised by the fineness of its fibres (see paragraph A2.28), which often are present in closely packed bundles of fibrils that will divide along their length when pressure is exerted on them with a probe or tweezers. A competent analyst will be familiar with characteristics such as distinctive surface lustre, flexibility and tensile strength, as shown in Figure A2.2. Initial tentative identification of the fibres at this stage will be confirmed or refuted by subsequent examination using PLM.

Preparation of samples for PLM

A2.22 A tentative identification based on the stereo microscopy evaluation is used to select the most appropriate RI mounting liquid. Fibres should be dry and relatively free from other particulate matter. Representative fibres or fibre bundles are chosen and are placed on a clean microscope slide into a drop of RI liquid, and a clean cover slip is lowered gently onto the slide. The RI of the liquid selected should be close to one of the two observable fibre RIs (see paragraph A2.40 and Table A2.3) for positive identification (for example 1.550 for chrysotile, 1.670 for amosite and 1.700 for crocidolite).

A2.23 For bulk samples in which no fibres have been seen using the stereo microscope, or no asbestos fibres have been identified by PLM, tweezers or probes should be used to take random sub-samples after the bulk sample has undergone suitable treatment (if necessary). At least two microscope slide preparations should be made with appropriate RI liquids for examination by PLM. Any large agglomerates should be teased apart, or may be ground gently between two microscope slides, to give an even distribution. Selection of large particles or fibre bundles may cause tilting of the cover slip and should be avoided. The amount of sample distributed should be such that the appearance and properties of individual fibres are not obscured by other particles.

Asbestos identification by PLM

A2.24 Identification of a single asbestos fibre requires the assessment of the following properties in the stated observation modes.

Property	Observation mode
(a) Morphology	All modes
(b) Colour and pleochroism (if present)	Polariser only
(c) Birefringence (anisotropic behaviour)	Crossed polars
(d) Extinction characteristics	Crossed polars
(e) Sign of elongation	Crossed polars with first order red compensator
(f) RI assessment	Normally using a dispersion staining, or phase contrast, objective with polariser only

The above order facilitates the assessment of the listed properties in a logical sequence. The microscope is adjusted to give Köhler illumination, the stage is centred, and a polariser (usually adjusted to the E-W position) is inserted below the condenser. Under these conditions morphology, colour and (with stage rotation) pleochroism can be observed. The analyser is then inserted (to give crossed-polars) and the stage is rotated to observe birefringence and the extinction characteristics. With the polars still crossed, a first order red compensator is inserted and the stage is rotated to determine the sign of elongation. Finally the RIs of the fibre are assessed by dispersion staining to see whether

Table A2.2 Use of physical properties and appearance under the stereo microscope to determine choice of RI liquid for PLM identification of asbestos fibre type

Physical property/appearance						
Colour	Colourless/white	Colourless/white to grey brown			Greenish-grey deep blue	
Texture	Soft with bundles of sinuous fibres	Soft or harsh; may appear as easily visible parallel fibre bundles			Soft or harsh with parallel fibre bundles	
Appearance	Flexible fibres which cling to tweezers	Straight fibres easy to handle			Straight fibres easy to handle	
Lustre	Silky	Vitreous	Vitreous	Vitreous	Vitreous	Metallic (dark and highly reflective)
Tensile strength	High	High	Medium	Low	Low	High
Tenacity	Flexible	Flexible	Flexible	Flexible	Flexible	Flexible
Elasticity	Inelastic	Elastic	Elastic	Elastic	Elastic	Elastic
Tentative asbestos type	Chrysotile	Amosite	Antho-phyllite	Tremolite	Actinolite	Crocidolite
RI liquid for test	1.550	1.670	1.605	1.605	1.640	1.700

or not the values are typical and consistent with published data. This may be achieved by observing the dispersion colours at the interface between the fibre and the RI liquid; the most commonly used techniques require that the analyser and compensator be withdrawn, the illumination be increased, and an objective with a central stop or phase ring in the back focal plane be inserted together with an appropriate condenser stop (paragraphs A2.13 and A2.39).

A2.25 **In practice any other sequence may be used provided that all of the properties are observed under the correct conditions.** For instance, if it is difficult to find the fibres on the prepared mount, or the sample is dominated by non-asbestos fibres, or a random sample is being searched, the sample should be scanned with the microscope in modes (c), (d), (e) or (f) above to detect the asbestos fibres.

A2.26 The observations made of the morphology and the optical properties of the fibre are recorded. Identification is based on comparing the recorded observations on the fibres selected for analysis (and mounted in the appropriate RI liquid) against the properties of asbestos reference standards (which may be in the form of a table such as Table A2.3, derived from such standards). A close match between the optical properties of the sample fibre and the asbestos standard will normally be achieved. Further representative fibres will need to be analysed if the observations are inconclusive, or if more than one type of fibre was found in the stereo or PLM analysis.

A2.27 An example of a suitable analytical sequence is given in Figure A2.1. Optical properties of asbestos are summarised in Table A2.3, and more detailed descriptions of the optical properties required to positively identify asbestos minerals follow in paragraphs A2.28-A2.40. Details of the technique by which these properties may be best observed by the analyst are also included. Common problems that arise during identification are discussed in paragraphs A2.41-A2.53. Descriptions of the physics behind the modes of operation, and of the optical properties observed, are beyond the scope of this method and can be found in various standard texts.[56, 57]

Morphology

A2.28 The amphibole minerals which form asbestos also occur in non-fibrous forms.[58] These non-fibrous forms are listed in Table A2.1 and can occur as, or be broken into, fragments which are long and thin, some of which may satisfy the regulatory definition for fibre counting.[5] However, the asbestos regulations only apply to the asbestos forms of the minerals. (Studies indicate that the biological potencies of such non-fibrous forms are lower than for the asbestos forms of the minerals).[59] In recent years a more detailed description for asbestiform morphology has been developed and appears in the literature.[60, 61] This is reproduced below and can be used to distinguish between populations of asbestos fibres and non-asbestiform fragments (see also paragraphs A2.42 and A2.43):

'Under a light microscope, the asbestiform habit is generally recognised by the following characteristics:

■ a range of aspect ratios ranging from 20:1 to 100:1 or higher for fibres longer than 5 µm;
■ capability of splitting into very thin fibrils;
■ two or more of the following:
  - *parallel fibres occurring in bundles;*
  - *fibre bundles displaying frayed ends;*
  - *fibres in the form of thin needles;*
  - *matted masses of individual fibres; and/or*
  - *fibres showing curvature.'*

Table A2.3 Properties used to identify asbestos by PLM

Asbestos type		Chrysotile	Amosite	Anthophyllite	Tremolite	Actinolite	Crocidolite
RI liquid *Property*		1.550	1.670	1.605	1.605	1.640	1.700
Morphology	Fibrous	Fibrous	Fibrous	Fibrous	Fibrous	Fibrous	Fibrous
Pleochroism	Fibre parallel	None	None	None	None	Green	Blue
	Fibre perpendicular	None	None	None	None	Grey	Grey
Birefringence		Low	Moderate	Moderate	Moderate	Moderate	Low/ anomalous
Extinction		Complete, or undulose with curved fibres; parallel	Complete; parallel	Complete; parallel	Complete; parallel or small angle	Complete; parallel or small angle	Complete; parallel
Sign of elongation		Usually positive (length slow)	Positive (length slow)	Positive (length slow)	Positive (length slow)	Positive (length slow)	Usually negative (length fast)
Dispersion staining	Fibre parallel	Purple	Yellow	Yellow-orange	Yellow	Yellow-brown	Blue
Objective colours	Fibre perpendicular	Blue	Purple-red	Blue-red	Blue	Blue-purple	Blue
Phase contrast	Fibre parallel Fibre colour Halo colour	Pale-blue Orange	Grey Yellow	Dark-grey Orange	Dark-grey Yellow	Dark-grey Yellow	Blue Red-brown
Objective colours	Fibre perpendicular Fibre colour Halo colour	Pale-blue Orange	Blue Orange	Blue Orange-yellow	Blue Orange	Blue Orange	Blue Red-brown
Refractive	$n\alpha$	1.537-1.554*	1.670-1.675*	1.596-1.654+	1.599-1.620+	1.619-1.658+	1.680-1.692*
Index ranges	$n\gamma$	1.545-1.557	1.683-1.694*	1.625-1.667+	1.622-1.641+	1.641-1.677+	1.683-1.700*

(Note: Fibre parallel or fibre perpendicular describes orientation with respect to the polariser. Dispersion colours relate to the HSE reference standards.[55] Slight compositional variations will give rise to differences in the dispersion staining colours observed. RI ranges marked * were obtained from commercial asbestos fibre;[62] RI ranges marked + were obtained from non-commercial fibres).[63]

Colour and pleochroism

A2.29 Colour and pleochroism are observed using plane polarised light. Pleochroism is defined as a change in colour of the fibre with orientation relative to the vibration plane of polarised light. Crocidolite has a natural strong absorption, which gives a dark blue colour when parallel to the polariser, changing to pale blue-grey when perpendicular, as the fibre is rotated. Actinolite often has a natural green colour and changes from green parallel to the polariser to pale green, grey or yellow when perpendicular to the polariser. These properties are important in the identification of crocidolite and actinolite (Table A2.3). The other four asbestos types show little colour contrast under plane polarised light, unless exposed to heat (paragraph A2.44).

A2.30 Alternatively, pleochrosim can be detected by orienting a fibre at 45° between crossed polars. The colour of the fibre is observed as the polariser (or analyser) is rotated a small angle each way from the crossed polar position. Any difference in colour between the two directions of rotation indicates that the fibre is pleochroic.[56] This is a very sensitive test of pleochroism, and is convenient to perform when observing birefringence and angle of extinction using crossed polars.

Birefringence

A2.31 The numerical difference between the highest and lowest RIs of a mineral is known as the birefringence. When a particle with more than one RI is observed between crossed polars with its planes of vibration at 45° to those of the polariser, interference colours are observed against the dark background. For asbestos these interference colours depend on the fibre thickness, and on birefringence.

A2.32 Between crossed polars, an asbestos fibre aligned at 45° to the polariser vibration direction should be clearly visible. Chrysotile has low birefringence and gives a grey colour for thin fibres, and a white colour or sometimes higher first (or even second) order colours for thick fibres. Crocidolite has a low birefringence and strong pleochroism which results in anomalous interference colours from grey to pale blue or sometimes a brown. The other amphibole asbestos fibres have moderate birefringence, giving white interference colours for thin fibres and higher first or second order colours for thick fibres. Fibres with a variable thickness, for example with wedge shaped cross-sections, will show parallel bands of colour along their lengths representing lower interference colours for the progressively thinner sections.

A2.33 Isotropic materials do not polarise the light transmitted through them and therefore are distinguished easily from asbestos. Between crossed polars such isotropic materials (for example man-made mineral fibres) are barely visible, but will be seen more easily with the first-order red compensator in place, or with slightly uncrossed polars. Interference colours can be used to distinguish asbestos from some natural organic fibres, which may show non-uniform interference along the fibre and incomplete extinction.

Angle of extinction

A2.34 As the microscope stage is rotated through 360°, an asbestos fibre viewed between crossed polars will disappear from view or 'extinguish' at four positions each 90° apart, while at 45° between each extinction interference colours should be visible. Many fibres, including asbestos, generally show complete extinction when parallel to the vibration planes of the polariser or the analyser. Chrysotile, amosite, crocidolite and anthophyllite show straight or parallel extinction when the fibre is parallel to the vibration orientation of the polariser or analyser (which are at right angles to each other and normally aligned E-W or N-S respectively). Actinolite and tremolite asbestos exhibit parallel or very nearly parallel (less than 5° from parallel) extinction (see also paragraphs A2.42 and A2.43).

Sign of elongation

A2.35 The sign of elongation describes the relationship between fibre shape and optical properties. The two available vibration orientations are parallel to the long axis and perpendicular to it. If the high RI vibration plane (slow ray) is parallel to the long axis, then the fibre is described as positive (or length slow); if the low RI vibration plane (fast ray) is parallel to the long axis, the fibre is described as negative (or length fast). Between crossed polars, with the first order red compensator inserted at 45°, the sign of elongation can be determined by observing the colours of fibres which previously had given grey or white first order interference colours between crossed polars. For a compensator with the slow direction (usually marked) in the NE-SW direction, the colours observed are as follows:

- Positive (length slow) fibre — blue-green with fibre NE-SW, orange-yellow with fibre NW-SE

- Negative (length fast) fibre — orange-yellow with fibre NE-SW, blue-green with fibre NW-SE

Crocidolite is the only one of the six regulated asbestos types which generally has negative sign of elongation (length fast). However, exposure to heat of about 300°C or higher may change the sign of elongation of crocidolite to positive (length slow); see paragraph A2.44.

Figure A2.2 HSE asbestos reference samples viewed by polarised light microscopy

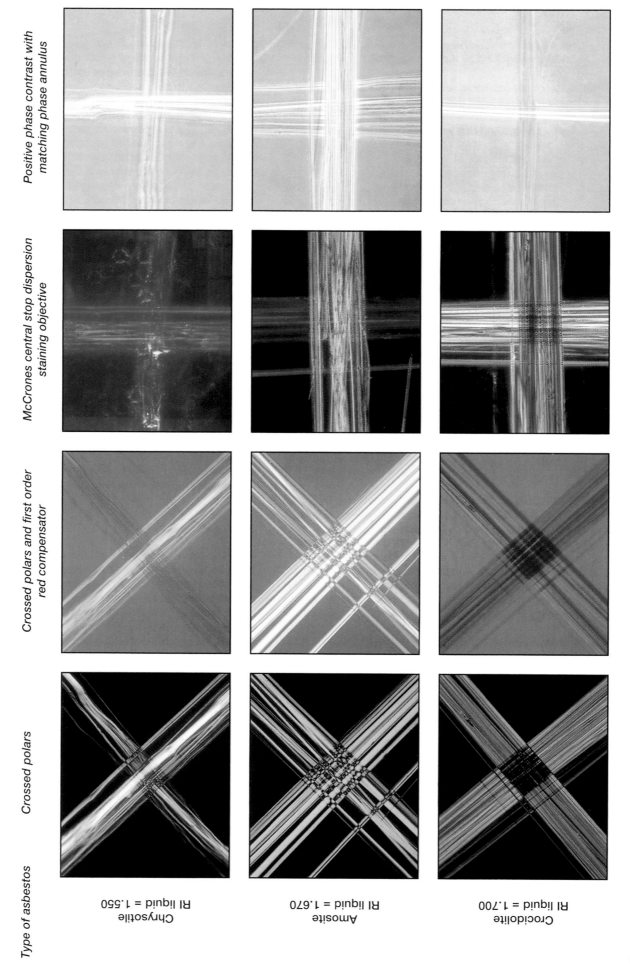

Type of asbestos	Crossed polars	Crossed polars and first order red compensator	McCrones central stop dispersion staining objective	Positive phase contrast with matching phase annulus
Chrysotile RI liquid = 1.550				
Amosite RI liquid = 1.670				
Crocidolite RI liquid = 1.700				

For a compensator with the slow direction in the NE-SW orientation and polariser aligned in the E-W direction. All phase contrast dispersion mounts used the Series B (1.556, 1.680, 1.692, 1.640, 1.604, 1.604) RI liquids, and McCrones central stop dispersion staining mounts used the Series E high dispersion RI liquids (as given). Approximate magnification is X 100.

Figure A2.2 HSE asbestos reference samples viewed by polarised light microscopy (cont)

Colour and pleochroism in plane polarised light

Crocidolite
RI liquid = 1.700

Positive phase contrast with matching phase annulus

Type of asbestos McCrones central stop dispersion staining objective

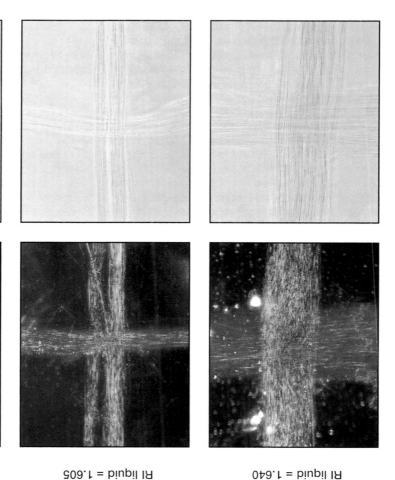

Anthophyllite
RI liquid = 1.605

Tremolite
RI liquid = 1.605

Actinolite
RI liquid = 1.640

For a compensator with the slow direction in the NE-SW orientation and polariser aligned in the E-W direction. All phase contrast dispersion mounts used the Series B (1.556, 1.680, 1.692, 1.640, 1.604, 1.604) RI liquids, and McCrones central stop dispersion staining mounts used the Series E high dispersion RI liquids (as given). Approximate magnification is X 100.

Note: crossed polars and crossed polars with a first order compensator plate appearances for anthophyllite, tremolite and actinolite are the same as for amosite.

Refractive index (RI)

A2.36 The RIs of an asbestos fibre are assessed by mounting the clean separated fibre in a liquid of known RI and orienting it either parallel or perpendicular to the polariser vibration direction. One or more observations are conducted to determine whether the RI of the fibre is higher than, lower than or equal to, that of the mounting liquid. The types of observation that can be made are:

■ relief;
■ Becke line;
■ dispersion staining colours.

Dispersion staining colours alone is sufficient if a phase contrast or a dispersion staining objective is used and the fibre is mounted in a liquid close to RI match point so that dispersion staining colours can be observed. When dealing with an atypical sample, relief and Becke line are simple observations which can be used to choose a suitable mounting liquid such that the RIs of fibre and liquid are close to match point.

Relief

A2.37 Relief is the term used in microscopy to describe visible contrast between a particle and its mounting medium. The greater the relief, the greater the RI difference between the particle and the mounting liquid. Therefore, if the correct RI liquid has been chosen, little relief should be present and it may be difficult to find asbestos fibres using plane polarised light. If high relief is observed, there is little point in trying to observe dispersion staining colours and a different RI liquid mount should be prepared. It should be noted that relief can be increased by partially closing the condenser iris.

Becke line

A2.38 When high relief is observed, it is important to know whether a higher or lower RI liquid should be tried. Partially closing the condenser iris to give an axial beam will result in refraction of the light owing to the differences in RI between the liquid and the particle, forming a bright halo at the edge of the particle. To determine whether the particle has a higher or lower RI than the mounting liquid, the movement of the halo is observed as the focus is lowered or raised. In most microscopes the stage is moved: when the stage is lowered (the equivalent of a raised focus) the halo or Becke line moves towards the medium with the higher RI. For fine fibres the effect is best observed using a high magnification objective. When the RIs of the liquid and particles are close, dispersion causes two Becke lines to appear; the red line moves into the particle and the blue line moves into the liquid.

Dispersion staining

A2.39 Dispersion is a term used to describe the variation in RI with the wavelength of light. Differences in dispersion between particles and liquids mean that even though the RIs match at one wavelength, they may be quite different at others. This leads to colour effects when fibres are observed in matching RI liquids using white light. It is easiest to observe small bright particles against a black background; hence a central stop in the back focal plane of the objective is used with an axial beam of light produced by the condenser iris.[51] Another method which produces a coloured image on a grey background, is to use a phase contrast objective with a corresponding phase annulus in the condenser. In both cases, the colours observed depend on the precise wavelength at which RIs for the liquids and fibres match. Dispersion staining is a particularly valuable technique for routine identification of asbestos in commercially produced products.[51, 64]

■ Dispersion staining objective – central stop (saturated colours on a black background):

Fibre RI >>	Liquid RI	White
Fibre RI >	Liquid RI	Purple-red/Orange/Yellow
Fibre RI =	Liquid RI	Purple
Fibre RI <	Liquid RI	Blue/Blue-green
Fibre RI <<	Liquid RI	White

■ Positive phase contrast (desaturated colours on a grey background):

Fibre RI >	Liquid RI	Thin fibres darker than background; thick fibres can show light in centre of fibre with thin dark outline.
Fibre RI =	Liquid RI	Blue colour to fibre, with a diffuse red or orange halo.
Fibre RI <	Liquid RI	Thin fibres lighter than background; thick fibres can show dark shading in centre of fibre.

Where there is a mismatch of RI, phase contrast is particularly helpful in deciding whether the fibres are lower or higher RI than the liquid they have been mounted in.

A2.40 Different colours will be observed with the dispersion staining objective when the fibre is oriented parallel or perpendicular to the polariser, arising from the different RIs of asbestos fibres. Recording of the predominant colours is used to characterise the fibre RIs. In theory, the identification of commonly encountered asbestos fibres can be performed with a dispersion staining objective using five high dispersion liquids having the RI values 1.550 for chrysotile, 1.605 for tremolite and anthophyllite, 1.640 for actinolite, 1.670 for amosite and 1.700 for crocidolite. In practice, because of variations in the fibre composition according to source, a wider range of fibre RIs can be found and a more extensive range of RI liquids may be required to achieve RI match between fibre and liquid. Examples of the dispersion staining colours obtained with the HSE reference materials[22] are listed in Table A2.3 and illustrated in Figure A2.2.

Common problems

Positive identification of certain amphibole fibres

A2.41 To avoid mis-identification of the amphibole type, it is important that all the required observations are made and compared against observations made for reference asbestos fibres exhibiting properties such as those listed in Table A2.3. RI ranges in Table A2.3 have been taken from two literature sources: those quoted for chrysotile, amosite and crocidolite respectively were obtained from commercial asbestos fibres;[64] those quoted for anthophyllite, tremolite and actinolite were obtained from non-commercial asbestos fibres.[64] However, it should be noted that the optical properties alone may not be sufficient to distinguish between tremolite and actinolite from some sources (because these minerals are members of a 'solid solution series' for which there is continuously varying composition giving a continuous range of RIs),[51] or between tremolite and anthophyllite (because they have similar birefringence and RI ranges). When such distinctions are critical, additional methods of analysis (for example analytical electron microscopy, X-ray diffraction or infra-red spectroscopy) should be used (see also paragraph A2.4). If only PLM is available, examination of acicular non-asbestos forms of the associated minerals (which may be present in the sample) can be helpful in making the distinctions.

Differentiation between asbestos and elongated mineral fragments

A2.42 Amphibole minerals are often coarse with prismatic or lath-like crystals which tend to break along two sets (at 60° to each other) of parallel planes of weakness within the atomic lattice known as cleavage planes. As a result the dust produced tends to contain a number of elongated fragments having sizes within the definition of a regulated fibre (longer than 5 μm, diameter less than 3 μm and aspect ratio >3:1, as used for fibre counting).[5] These elongated fragments have important properties which distinguish them from asbestos.[58, 65] In some circumstances the analyst may need to identify elongated particles and decide whether they are mineral fragments or asbestos fibres. All of the non-asbestos amphibole minerals, including non-fibrous forms of anthophyllite, tremolite and actinolite, have three vibration planes and three different RIs. Anthophyllite is orthorhombic and hence exhibits parallel extinction. The other relevant amphiboles are monoclinic and (depending on crystal orientation) this can result in extinction occurring when the elongated crystal axis forms an angle up to 20° with the vibration directions of the crossed polars. If a crystal exhibiting maximum extinction angle is reoriented about its long axis, it will show parallel extinction.

A2.43 Asbestos fibres are mineralogically anomalous in effectively showing only two RI vibration planes and consistent parallel extinction. [58, 59, 65] This is because even the very thin fibres that can be viewed in the polarised light microscope consist of bundles of polyfilamentous crystals with each crystallite randomly oriented along the length of the bundle. The difference between the extinction characteristics, together with the fibrous morphology described in paragraph A2.28, is used as the basis of the polarised light microscopy discrimination between asbestos and amphibole mineral fragments.

Heated asbestos[48-51]

A2.44 Certain changes occur when asbestos is progressively heated. Therefore care should be taken if sample preparation involves heating the asbestos-containing material. Prolonged exposure to temperatures of 300-500°C of crocidolite and amosite causes colour changes, and increases in both RIs and the birefringence. For crocidolite, the changes with heating are: the sign of elongation reverses and the colour changes through grey then yellow to orange-brown; pleochroism is suppressed at the grey colouration stage, but reappears on further heating. For amosite the sign of elongation remains positive (length slow) but the colour changes through yellow to a dark brown, and pleochroism is observed. Thus, heat degraded crocidolite and amosite are effectively indistinguishable by light microscopy after exposure to temperatures above about 500°C. The RIs of chrysotile increase after significant exposure to temperatures of about 600°C or greater: the birefringence decreases, and in a few cases the sign of elongation changes to negative (length fast) and the fibres become pale brown. The alteration of asbestos by heat is dependent upon both the duration and the temperature of exposure. Prolonged exposure to high temperatures can result in complete degradation (for example, of furnace linings) but with judicious sampling unaffected fibres can often be detected in peripheral locations or in debris which became detached during installation.

Fibres with morphological and/or optical properties similar to asbestos

A2.45 Most of the fibres discussed in the following paragraphs occur infrequently in samples presented for analysis. However, analysts need to be aware of their existence and distinguishing characteristics in PLM. Five types of fibre which can resemble chrysotile are discussed in paragraphs A2.46 to A2.50. Some mineral fibres which superficially resemble amphiboles are discussed in paragraphs A2.51 to A2.53.

A2.46 Polyethylene is the most important of the interfering fibres because it is used as an asbestos substitute. Shredded polyethylene resembles chrysotile.[51] In RI liquid 1.550 the fibres show dispersion stain with colours which appear typical of chrysotile (although more experienced analysts will observe desaturation of the blue colour across the fibres because of the low RI in this direction). The birefringence is higher than that of chrysotile, but the fibres are thin and hence generally show only first order white interference colours. If polyethylene is suspected, the melting of fibres on a hot plate or in a flame will distinguish them from chrysotile.

A2.47 Leather swarf fibres have low birefringence and similar dispersion stained colours to chrysotile.[66] At low magnification (X 100) they appear to have similar morphology to chrysotile, but they usually have clearly visible uniform fibrils. Chrysotile fibrils are too small to be seen by PLM, although less uniform bundles of fibrils (fibres) are visible. In most instances the differences between chrysotile and leather swarf can be detected during examination with the low power stereo microscope: the material handles differently during examination under the stereo microscope. If leather is suspected as being present, the sample may be ashed at 400°C to remove it, and then re-examined for identification of asbestos. Care should be taken not to let the sample temperature rise above 600°C (see paragraph A2.44).

A2.48 Macerated aramid fibres may appear to have a morphology similar to chrysotile but are recognisable by their extreme birefringence showing high order white interference colours. When mounted in RI liquid 1.640 they will show highly variable relief as the stage is rotated, because the lowest RI (across the fibre) is close to 1.64, while the higher RI (along the fibre) is of the order 2.4.

A2.49 Spiders' webs, and natural organic fibres such as paper and feathers, have RIs close to those of chrysotile and show similar interference colours between crossed polars. In a clean sample, the morphology will distinguish them from chrysotile. However, in a sample containing a lot of particulates, sometimes only a small portion of fibre can be observed due to obscuration by the particles and this can lead to misidentification. Again these fibres can be removed by ashing the sample or exposing individual fibres to a flame (but refer to paragraph A2.53 for changes to asbestos which may occur on heating).

A2.50 Talc fibres are thin ribbons which may be recognised by characteristic morphological twists and kinked bent forms. They have a higher RI than chrysotile parallel to the fibre length (in the range 1.589 to 1.600, giving a dispersion staining colour pale yellow in RI liquid 1.550). The other two RIs of talc are in the ranges 1.539 to 1.550 and 1.589 to 1.600,[3] and are observed perpendicular to the fibre, at different orientations as the fibre is 'rolled' (with a dispersion staining objective, blue and pale yellow in RI liquid 1.550).

A2.51 Fibrous Brucite (Nemalite) normally consists of straight white to pale brown fibres but lacks the tensile strength of asbestos, is brittle and is soluble in acid.[51] It has a negative sign of elongation (length fast) which reverses to positive (length slow) when heated. It is distinguished from asbestos by its RIs which are in the range 1.560 to 1.590 parallel to the fibre and 1.580 to 1.600 perpendicular[3] (with central stop dispersion staining giving colours of yellow to pale yellow in RI liquid 1.550, or pale blue in RI liquid 1.605).

A2.52 Fibrous Wollastonite has an acicular morphology,[51] is very brittle, white in appearance and soluble in acid. It has RIs which overlap with tremolite, actinolite and anthophyllite although it has lower birefringence and always displays an extinction angle. The RI almost parallel to the fibre is in the range 1.628 to 1.650. The other two RIs are in the ranges 1.626 to 1.640, and 1.631 to 1.653, and are observed across the fibre, at different orientations as the fibre is rolled.[51] A distinctive feature is that the RI along the fibre is

Table A2.4 Maximum numbers of samples of each type that can be analysed in a 24 hour period by a single analyst before implementing additional quality checks

Type of ACM	Maximum number of samples per 24 hours for an analyst
Asbestos cement (AC)	40
Asbestos insulating board (AIB)	40
Floor tiles (thermoplastic)	40
Bituminous products (eg roofing felt, damp proof courses, mastics, glues and thermoplastic floor tiles)	40
Laggings (preformed/friable)	40
Sprayed and loose fill asbestos	40
Textiles and gaskets	40
Hard set lagging	20
Decorative plaster/textured coatings/paints	20
Vinyl floor tiles	20
Soils containing asbestos	20
Asbestos impurities in mineral products	20

Note: To calculate analyses of various types of ACM, eg 1 vinyl floor tile analysis = 2 asbestos cement analysis, so a combined total of 10 floor tile analyses plus 20 asbestos cement analyses can be carried out, before increasing the quality control reanalysis to 20%

intermediate between the two RIs observed at the different orientations across the fibre as the fibre is rolled. Thus examination of many fibres with crossed polars and first order red compensator will show most as length slow (as the fibre is lath-like and has a preferred orientation); other orientations may appear as length fast. Gentle pressure on the coverslip with a needle can be used to rotate a fibre and show it to appear both length fast and length slow.

A2.53 Diatomaceous earth may show acicular fragments with the appearance of fibres. However, the low RI of 1.42 will easily distinguish them from asbestos fibres using dispersion staining techniques. The characteristic morphology is recognised at magnifications around X 500.

Identification of other sample components

A2.54 A laboratory conducting routine analysis selectively removes fibres for examination and ignores the majority of the non-asbestos materials. The composition of many asbestos products is relatively uniform during manufacture and a wider knowledge of materials identification can be helpful in recognising many common products or formulations.

Quality assurance (QA) and quality control (QC)

A2.55 A routine QA programme to assess the quality of the results produced by the PLM laboratory must be developed and implemented. The purpose of a QA programme is to ensure that the sampling, analysis, recording and reporting of the results all meet acceptable standards. A QA programme will usually have a written protocol to describe how each stage of the procedure is conducted and will define the types of QC measurements and checks that are required. Many of the required procedures are covered in the UKAS Accreditation Scheme for asbestos sampling and identification.[20] From 21 November 2004 laboratories carrying out this work must be accredited by UKAS.

A2.56 The performance of the analyst will be affected if large numbers of bulk samples are analysed daily. The time needed to analyse a sample will vary with the sample type. Often to report that no asbestos was detected in a sample will take longer than to positively identify the asbestos types present in many ACMs. If the total number of samples analysed in a 24-hour period exceed the numbers given in Table A2.4 additional quality checks must be carried out. At least 20% of the excess samples should be reanalysed, preferably by a second analyst, once the maximum number has been exceeded. The QC samples must represent the types of materials analysed.

A2.57 Laboratory performance testing is necessary to confirm that the analyst can maintain performance with time, and standards should be set to measure whether or not analytical performance is adequate to meet the quality objectives of the laboratory. Various ways in which intra-laboratory performance can be monitored are described in other HSE guidance (MDHS71).[67] The Asbestos in Materials (AIMS) scheme is an international inter-laboratory proficiency testing scheme designed to measure the performance of laboratories which analyse asbestos in bulk materials (see

'Suppliers of equipment and services'). Laboratories are required to participate and maintain satisfactory performance in the AIMS scheme. Ideally, performance testing should be conducted 'blind' and should involve everyday commercial samples, along with the less common asbestos types and fibrous materials which resemble asbestos, as well as the three main commercial asbestos minerals.

A2.58 Microscopes and ancillary equipment must be maintained in good order, and alignment checks should be conducted prior to analysis. RI liquids can become contaminated through improper use, resulting in a change of RI or the introduction of fibres from samples. Routine monitoring checks for contamination should be performed and recorded[20] (see also paragraph A2.10).

A2.59 Training is of fundamental importance to both sampling and analysis. If an asbestos building survey is conducted, the training and experience of the sampler will control the quality of the survey. Microscopic determination of asbestos requires the analyst to make repeated assessments of a number of physical properties and maintain consistent diligence in the search for fibres. Many of the procedures rely on the quality of judgement of the analyst as well as correct use and alignment of the microscope and detailed recording of the properties tested. Analysts should be thoroughly familiar with the appearance and characteristics of asbestos when viewed by a stereo microscope, and by the various modes of operation of the polarised light microscope. Ideally, the analyst should have specialised training in asbestos identification. Also, experience is very important and until analysts are fully trained, all their analyses should be checked by an experienced analyst. An adequate laboratory QA programme will contain detailed descriptions of the training programme, together with the training records of each analyst. The minimum requirement is that an analyst must be able to identify representative (well-defined) fibres of the six regulated asbestos types. Reference fibre standards have been prepared on behalf of HSE for this requirement.[55] Contact HSL for further information. In addition, samples chosen for the training programme should typify the range of materials analysed by the laboratory.

A2.60 Colour or other vision defects need not disqualify a prospective analyst, provided that the individual is able to properly assess the optical characteristics described in this method, and achieve a satisfactory standard of performance in a quality assurance scheme. An HSE Medical Series Guidance Note MS7 on colour vision[68] is available, which includes a list of colour vision tests. (The most recently developed is the 'City University' test, 1973.) Currently, UKAS requires that all identification analysts undergo a suitable test (such as the Ishihara test).[20]

Advice

A2.61 Advice on this method may be obtained from the Minerals and Fibres Section, Health and Safety Laboratory (see 'Further information' for the address). Suggestions for improvement should also be sent to this address.

Sample packaging and transport

A2.62 Bulk samples of asbestos materials taken on site will usually have to be transported to the laboratory for analysis. Asbestos samples are subject to labelling and packaging requirements in accordance with Schedule 2 of CAWR 2002[10] and the Carriage of Dangerous Goods and Use of Transportable Pressure Receptacles Regulations 2004[69] (CDG). CAWR 2002[10] requires asbestos items to be contained in 'sealed containers' which should bear the appropriate warning label, which is shown in Figure A2.3. In addition CDG requires all forms of asbestos to be contained in UN approved packaging (as detailed in Box A2.1) unless they are exempted under the exemptions listed in paragraphs A2.63 and A2.64.

Figure A2.3 Asbestos label

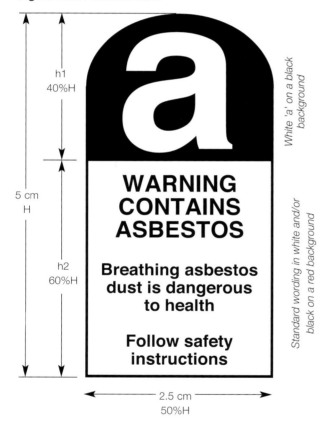

A2.63 Special Exemption 168 applies when asbestos fibres are either bonded or packaged in such a way that no fibres can become airborne in transit, namely:

- whole asbestos cement sheets that are transported in a sealed skip;
- articles with an asbestos component that cannot create airborne fibres in transit; eg a sealed fuse box containing asbestos rope or machinery with a sealed gasket;
- bonded materials such as bituminous floor tiles containing asbestos.

A2.64 The Limited Quantity (LQ) exemptions. There are specific exemptions for the different types of asbestos. For amphibole asbestos (UN reference number 2212) provision

LQ 25 applies. This means that fit for purpose 'inner packaging' of up to 1 kg asbestos may be carried in outer packagings of up to 4 kg. The following outer packagings are allowed:

- steel or aluminium drums with removable heads;
- steel or aluminium jerricans with removable heads;
- plywood or fibre drums;
- plastic drums or jerricans with removable heads;
- boxes of natural wood, plywood, reconstituted wood, fibreboard, plastic, steel or aluminium.

For chrysotile asbestos (UN reference number 2590) provision LQ 27 applies. The same LQ 25 packaging arrangements apply but the quantities are 6 kg and 24 kg for inner and outer packaging respectively.

A2.65 Asbestos samples are likely to qualify for an exemption from the CDG packaging requirements under the LQ exemptions or, in specific cases, under the bonded materials exemption. In practice, asbestos samples should be double bagged (with the bags individually sealed) and then placed in an allowed outer packaging, which bears the asbestos warning label (see Figure A2.3).

Asbestos waste

A2.66 CAW 2002[10] defines asbestos waste as being any amphibole or chrysotile asbestos that has been removed from its original place of use. The Environmental Protection Act (EPA) 1990[70] and associated regulations classifies construction and demolition waste as 'controlled waste' of which there are two types:

- special waste: waste that contains 0.1% (w/w) or more asbestos;
- non-special waste: waste containing up to 0.1% (w/w) asbestos.

A2.67 Asbestos samples are not considered to be special waste until there is an intention to discard them. Therefore asbestos samples are not special waste until they have been analysed and/or are to be discarded without analysis. Asbestos samples therefore can be collected and transported by the analyst without the need for a registered waste carrier until the samples are ready for disposal. When the intention is to dispose of the samples, it may be possible to return the sample to the client for disposal or, if this is not the case, it will be necessary to use a registered waste carrier to take them to a licensed tip using the relevant environment agency procedures.

A2.68 All movements of special waste must be consigned in accordance with the requirements of the Special Waste Regulations 1996.[71] A consignment note is required for all waste over 10 kg and all waste irrespective of amount must be transported by a registered waste carrier. More details of the requirements are available from the Environment Agency (EA) or the Scottish Environment Protection Agency (SEPA). The agencies can be contacted via the following websites: www.environment-agency.gov.uk and www.sepa.org.uk. The Special Waste Regulations are due to be revised in mid-2005.

Transport of asbestos waste

A2.69 The CDG Regulations stipulate a number of requirements for the transportation of asbestos waste materials. However there are exemptions to some of the requirements where the asbestos materials do not exceed certain quantity thresholds. The weight limits are set at 333 kg for amphibole asbestos and 1000 kg for chrysotile asbestos. The more limited requirements are likely to apply for all asbestos waste sample situations. The limited requirements include that the vehicle must have the appropriate signage and that the package must be accompanied by information in writing indicating the nature of the hazard and the emergency information (tremcard). The driver must also be adequately trained.

Box A2.1 UN-approved asbestos waste packaging

It is the consignor's duty to ensure that dangerous substances are properly packaged and labelled.

'UN-approved' package have been subjected to tests to ensure their suitability to withstand the handling associated with road transport. They will usually need to be used in double layers (red sack inside clear sack for example) and have specified means of closure (eg by pvc tape or 'swan necking' and taping). These details should be obtained from the supplier.

Typically, approval details will be marked in the following way:

 5H4/Yx/S/**/GB/abcd

5H4 is the code for plastic film bags
Y   indicates suitability for packing group II and III
     substances (covers both relevant UN numbers)
x   represents the maximum weight of contents in kg
S   means use for solids only
**   last digits of year of manufacture
GB   is the country of certification (could be another
     country. Symbols match those for cars)
abcd represents the certificate number

The bags should also be marked with the asbestos symbol (see Figure A2.3) and the CDG hazard label (shown in Figure A2.4 below).

Figure A2.4

A glossary of terms

Term (and paragraph of first appearance)	*RMS Dictionary of Light Microscopy:*[40] Definition
Analyser (A2.12)	A polar used after the object (usually between the objective and the primary image plane) to determine optical effects produced by the object on the light, polarised or otherwise, with which it is illuminated.
Becke line (A2.38)	A bright line (due to refraction and/or diffraction) formed in the image at the boundary between media of different optical path lengths. It moves in the direction of the longer optical path when the distance between the objective and the object is increased. Note: this phenomenon is used to recognise relative differences in RI of two adjacent media, eg a particle and the surrounding medium; when the RIs are matched the Becke line disappears.
Bertrand lens (A2.12)	An intermediate lens which transfers an image of the back focal plane of the objective into the primary image plane; used for conoscopic observation in polarised light microscopy and for adjustment of the microscope illumination system especially with phase contrast microscopy.
Birefringence (A2.31)	The qualitative expression of the maximum difference in RI due to double refraction (symbol n).
Compensator (A2.12)	A retardation plate (sometimes of variable optical path length difference) used to measure the optical path length differences within an object.
Condenser (A2.12)	A part of the illumination system of the microscope which consists of one or more lenses (or mirrors) and their mounts, usually containing a diaphragm, and is designed to collect, control and concentrate radiation.
Dispersion staining (A2.39)	The microscopy of transparent objects which are in a mounting medium, the RI of which matches that of the object for a certain wavelength, but which has a distinctly higher dispersive power than the object. Under these conditions, both the object and the mounting medium appear coloured near their interfaces. The colour with which the object appears is distinctly different from that with which the mountant appears. The colours and their differences depend on the wavelength at which the RIs of the object and medium match and the kind of microscopy used; dispersion staining may be used in bright-field microscopy, the colour being concentrated in the Becke line, in dark ground microscopy or in phase-contrast microscopy.
Eyepiece (A2.12)	A lens system which is responsible for the angular magnification of the final virtual image formed by it from the primary image. This image is converted into a real image by the observer's eye or other converging lens system.
First order red (A2.12)	The characteristic reddish violet interference colour at approximately 530 nm retardation.

Focal plane (A2.13)	(a) a surface connecting all the points at which bundles of parallel rays entering an ideal converging lens cross on the other side of the lens, and thus containing a focal point; (b) a surface at right angles to the optical axis of a lens (or mirror) in which the image of an object lying at infinity is formed: it is one of the cardinal planes.
Focusing eyepiece (A2.12)	An eyepiece with a mechanism for focusing an (interchangeable) graticule or diaphragm mounted within it and coinciding with the primary image.
Iris (A2.12)	A diaphragm bounded by multiple leaves, usually metal, arranged so as to provide an opening of variable size which is adjustable by means of a control.
Köhler illumination (A2.12)	A method of illuminating objects in which an image of the source is projected by a collector into the plane of the aperture diaphragm in the front focal plane of the condenser. This latter, in turn, projects an image of an illuminated field diaphragm at the opening of the collector into the object plane.
Numerical aperture (A2.12)	A number (often symbolised by the letters NA) originally defined by Abbé for objectives and condenser. It is given by the expression 'n. sin u', where 'n' is the RI of the medium between the lens and the object and 'u' is half the angular aperture of the lens.
Objective (A2.12)	The first part of the imaging system, consisting of a lens, its mount, and any associated parts. It forms a primary image of the object.
Phase (A2.12)	Relative position in a cyclical or wave motion; it is expressed as an angle, one cycle or wavelength corresponding to 2π radians or to 360°.
Pleochroism (A2.29)	The property of an optically anisotropic medium by which it exhibits different brightness and/or colour in different directions of light propagation, or in different vibration directions, on account of variation in selective spectral absorption of transmitted light.
Polarised light (A2.3)	LIght in which there is only one vibration direction.
Polariser (A2.12)	A polar placed in the light path before the object.
Power (A2.3)	The ability of an optical system to produce a magnified image under specified working conditions (for example the optical fitting dimensions). The magnifying power is expressed as the lateral or angular magnification of the image under consideration.
Refractive index (A2.3)	The ratio of the speed of light (more exactly, the phase velocity) in a vacuum to that in a given medium (symbolised by the letter n or n').
Retardation (A2.12)	The slower propagation of a wavefront in a medium or high RI as compared with that in a medium of low RI.

Stage (microscope stage) (A2.12)	The platform, at right angles to the optical axis of the which carries the object. It is often fitted with mechanical movements (as in a mechanical stage) to allow easy positioning of the object in the 'x' and 'y' axis and movement along, and rotation about, the 'z' axis.
Stereo microscope (A2.3)	A binocular microscope in which the object is observed by each eye from a slightly different angle. Disparate image points will be imaged on corresponding points of the retina and thus cause stereoscopic perception.

Suppliers of equipment and services

Equipment/service	Supplier
Asbestos reference samples	Institute of Occupational Medicine Research Park North Riccarton Edinburgh EH14 4AP Tel: 0870 850 5131
Cargille refractive index liquids	McCrone Scientific Limited McCrone House 155A Leighton Road London NW5 2RD Tel: 0207 267 7199
Accreditation service	United Kingdom Accreditation Service (UKAS) 21-47 High Street Feltham Middlesex TW13 4UN Tel: 0208 917 8555 e-mail: info@ukas.com
Asbestos in materials scheme	AIMS Health and Safety Laboratory Harpur Hill Buxton Derbyshire SK17 9JN Tel: 01142 892 000 e-mail: hslinfo@hsl.gov.uk

Appendix 3: Template for certificate of reoccupation

Laboratory name:

Address:

Tel:

Fax:

e-mail:

UKAS logo and accreditation number:

Certificate of reoccupation (# certificate number and # issue number)			
Contract number:	Job number:	Reference number:	
UKAS accredited method/s used and disclaimers: (Note: Methods accredited by UKAS must have a disclaimer, if you are reporting outside the scope of the method)			
Name, address and contact information for the client			
Site address for clearance			
Areas to be assessed and brief description of works, including dates carried out			
Give attachment number if following are attached	Drawings/pictures of the area to be assessed	Plan of work/extracts from the plan of work	ASB5 notification form
Attachment number			

Name, address and contact information for the asbestos removal contractor		
Name and contact information for asbestos removal contractor's site supervisor		
Representative who will confirm start and acknowledge outcome		
Anticipated start of the assessment	Date:	Time:
Confirmed start for the assessment	Date:	Time:

Stage 1 of 4: Preliminary check of site condition and job completeness

1.1 Plan of work checked to confirm areas to be assessed. (Record any problems,differences, fixed installations or ACMs to remain)	
State 'yes' if the following are intact and operating (record the problem if not)	
1.2 Work areas	
1.3 Enclosures/air extraction	
1.4 Hygiene facilities	
State yes if the following areas and their immediate surroundings appear to be free of obvious asbestos debris and asbestos waste sacks (record the problem if not)	
1.5 Skip area/waste route	
1.6 Transit route	
1.7 Hygiene facilities	
1.8 Enclosure/work area	
(Note: 1.8 should also be free of unnecessary equipment. If no, or insufficient viewing panels are fitted, note this down and continue with the assessment, as the area inside the enclosure will be covered in section 2.2)	

Stage 1: Passed/failed   **Time:**   **Date:**   **Assessed by:**

Comments:

Signature of assessor:
(If failed, strike through remaining stages and get the representative to sign the acknowledgement box at the end)

Stage 2 of 4: Thorough visual inspection

Requirement	Yes/No	Comments
2.1 Airlock/baglock/enclosure are free of waste bags, materials and unnecessary equipment		
2.2 All ACMs have been completely removed from the underlying surfaces		
2.3 Interior surfaces inside the enclosure are free from debris and fine settled dust		

Stage 2: Passed/failed   **Time:**   **Date:**   **Assessed by:**

The airlock, baglock and enclosure were *free/not free* of visible asbestos waste, debris and surface dust

Comments:

Signature of assessor:
(If failed, strike through remaining stages and get the representative to sign the acknowledgement box at the end)

Stage 3 of 4: Clearance air monitoring inside the enclosure

Sampling information	Yes/No	Comments/values
3.1 All areas are dry		
3.2 Air movers off and sealed		
3.3 No evidence of lock down sprays		
3.4 Original floor surface uncovered		
3.5 Disturbance used (state type)		
3.6 Total time of disturbance	Minutes	
3.7 Area or volume of enclosure	m^2	m^3
3.8 Number of air samples collected		

(A drawing showing the sampling positions is included as attachment #)

Results	Set 1: Fibre conc. (f/ml)	Set 2: Fibre conc. (f/ml)	Set 3: Fibre conc. (f/ml)	Set 4: Fibre conc. (f/ml)
Sample 1				
Sample 2				
Sample 3				
Sample 4				
Sample 5				
Pass/fail				

Stage 3: Passed/failed   **Time:**   **Date:**   **Assessed by:**

The area is *not cleared/cleared* for the enclosure to be removed
Test details for the air monitoring are recorded in attachment #

Comments:

Signature of assessor:
(If failed, strike through remaining stage and get the representative to sign the acknowledgement box at the end)

Stage 4 of 4: Assessment of site for reoccupation (after the enclosure is removed)

Requirements	Yes/no	Comments
4.1 Former enclosure/work area and the immediate surrounding area are free from any visible debris, asbestos sacks and waste		
4.2 Transit route and waste routes are free from any asbestos debris, asbestos sacks and waste		
4.3 All ACMs in the scope of work have been removed and any known ACMs remaining are intact		

Stage 4: Passed/failed   **Time:**   **Date:**   **Assessed by:**

The area can be/cannot be reoccupied

Comments:

Signature:

Contractor's representative acknowledgement:

I have been advised by   that the certificate of reoccupation has not been issued

because the area has failed stage #

I have been advised by   that the certificate of reoccupation can be issued as the area

has passed all four stages

(Complete one of the above and strike through the other option)

Name: Signature: Date: Time:

Issue of certificate of reoccupation by the assessor:

Copies of this certificate (certificate number and issue number) were issued with attachments # - # to the following people:

Name of Assessor: Signature: Date: Time:

Notes: A copy of the certificate must always be issued to the asbestos removal contractor. A separate clearance certificate of inspection for the hygiene facility is required by the asbestos removal contractor

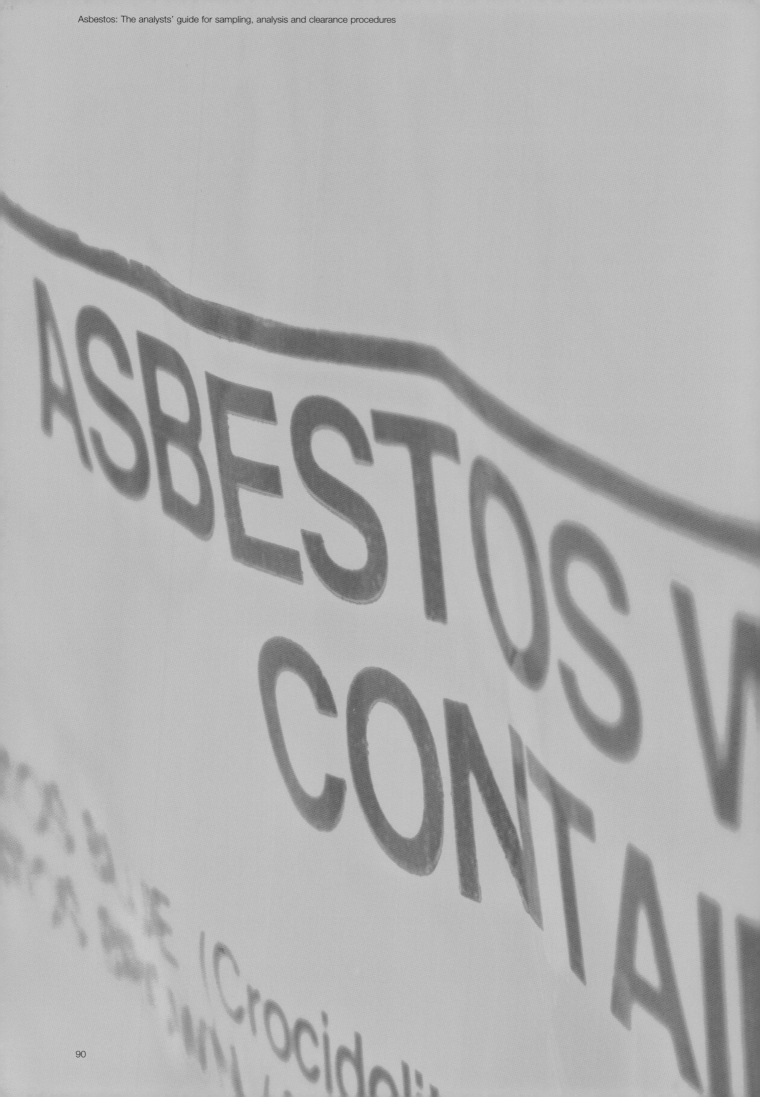

Appendix 4: Template for the inspection certificate for the hygiene facility

Laboratory name/Letterhead:

Address:

Tel:

Fax:

e-mail:

UKAS logo and accreditation number:

Certificate of inspection of hygiene facility (# certificate number and # issue number)		
Manufacturer:	Serial number:	
Contract number:	Job number:	Reference number:
UKAS accredited method(s) used and disclaimers: (Note: Methods accredited by UKAS must have a disclaimer if you are reporting outside the scope of the method)		
Name, address and contact information for the asbestos removal contractor		
Site address of the hygiene facility for clearance		
Name and contact information for asbestos removal contractor's site supervisor		
Representative who will confirm start and acknowledge outcome		
Anticipated start	Date:	Time:
Confirmed start	Date:	Time:

Thorough visual inspection		
Requirement	Yes/no	Comments
Hygiene facilities are free from waste, debris, dust, contaminated clothing, waste bags etc		
Interior surfaces are free from debris and settled dust		

Passed/failed inspection   Time: Date: Assessed by:

The hygiene facility *free/not free* of visible asbestos waste, debris and surface dust

Comments:

Signature of assessor:
(If failed, strike through remaining stages and get the representative to sign the acknowledgement box at the end)

Clearance air monitoring inside the hygiene facility		
Sampling information	Yes/no	Comments/values
All areas are dry		
Air movers off and sealed		
Disturbance used (state type)		
Total time of disturbance	Minutes	
Floor area of shower and dirty end of the hygiene facility	m^2	
Number of air samples collected		

Results of air monitoring			
Results	Set 1: Fibre conc. (f/ml)	Set 2: Fibre conc. (f/ml)	Set 3: Fibre conc. (f/ml)
Sample 1			
Sample 2			
Pass/fail			

Stage 3: Passed/failed   Time: Date: Assessed by:

The hygiene facility is *not cleared/cleared* for reuse
Test details for the air monitoring are recorded in attachment #

Comments:

Signature of assessor:

Contractor's representative acknowledgement:

I have been advised by   that an inspection certificate for the hygiene facility

can/cannot be issued

Name: Signature: Date: Time:

Issue of inspection certificate for the hygiene facility by the assessor:

Copies of this certificate (certificate number and issue number) **were issued to:**

Name of assessor ……………………………………Signature: ……………………………….. Date: Time:

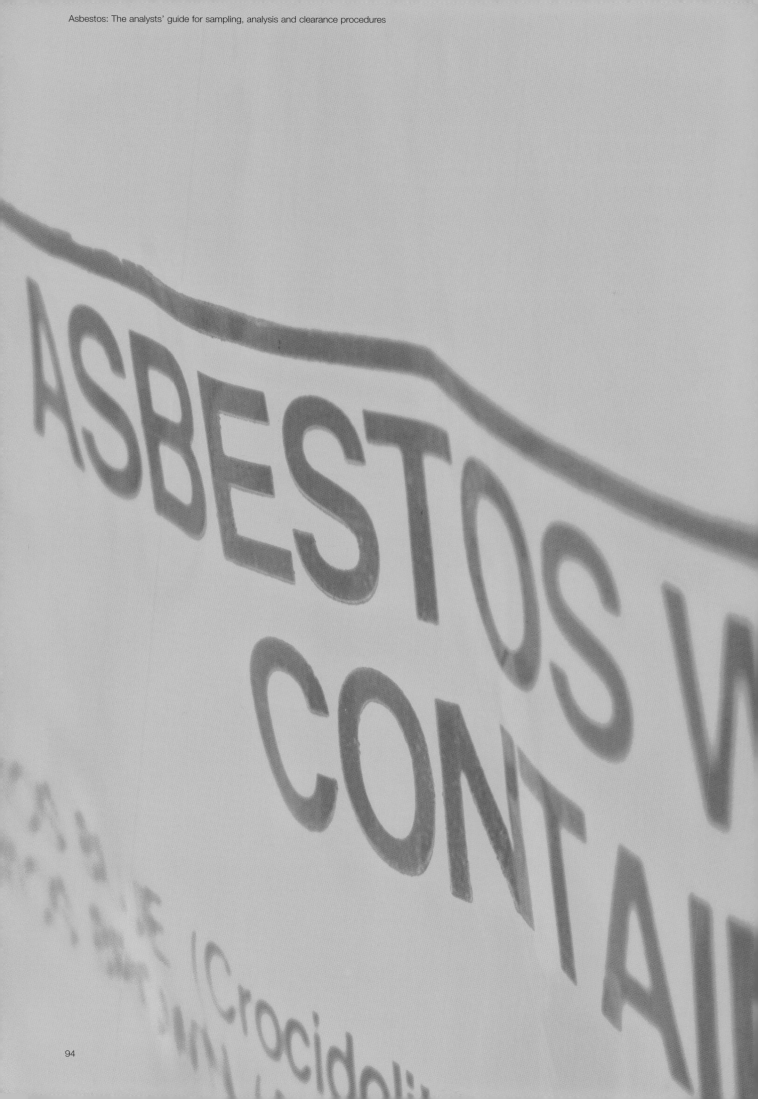

References and further information

References

1   *Asbestos essentials task manual: Task guidance sheets for the building maintenance and allied trades* HSG210 HSE Books 2001 ISBN 0 7176 1887 0

2   *Working with asbestos cement* HSG189/2 HSE Books 1999 ISBN 0 7176 1667 3

3   *Asbestos: The licensed contractors' guide* HSG247 HSE Books (Due for publication in 2005)

4   The protection of workers from the risks related to exposure to asbestos at work 2003/18/EC *Official Journal of the European Union* 2003

5   *Asbestos fibres in air: Sampling and evaluation by Phase Contrast Microscopy (PCM) under the Control of Asbestos at Work Regulations* MDHS39/4 (Fourth edition) HSE Books 1995 ISBN 0 7176 1113 2

6   *Determination of airborne fibre number concentrations: A recommended method, by phase-contrast optical microscopy (membrane filter method)* World Health Organisation 1997 ISBN 92 4154496 1

7   *Asbestos in bulk materials: Sampling and identification by polarised light microscopy (PLM)* MDHS77 HSE Books 1994 ISBN 0 7176 0677 5

8   *Surveying, sampling and assessment of asbestos-containing materials* MDHS100 HSE Books 2001 ISBN 0 7176 2076 X

9   *A comprehensive guide to managing asbestos in premises* HSG227 HSE Books 2002 ISBN 0 7176 2381 5

10   *Control of Asbestos at Work Regulations 2002* SI 2002/2675 The Stationery Office 2002 ISBN 0 11 042918 4

11   *Work with asbestos which does not normally require a licence. Control of Asbestos at Work Regulations 2002. Approved Code of Practice and guidance* L27 (Fourth edition) HSE Books 2002 ISBN 0 7176 2562 1

12   *Work with asbestos insulation, asbestos coating and asbestos insulating board. Control of Asbestos at Work Regulations 2002. Approved Code of Practice and guidance* L28 (Fourth edition) HSE Books 2002 ISBN 0 7176 2563 X

13   *The Asbestos (Licensing) Regulations 1983* SI 1983/1649 The Stationery Office 1983 ISBN 0 11 03764 9 as amended by *The Asbestos (Licensing) (Amendment) Regulations 1998* SI 1998/3233 The Stationery Office 1998 ISBN 0 11 080279 9

14   *The management of asbestos in non-domestic premises. Regulation 4 of the Control of Asbestos at Work Regulations 2002. Approved Code of Practice and guidance* L127 HSE Books 2002 ISBN 0 7176 2382 3

15   *Safety Representatives and Safety Committees Regulations 1977* SI 1977/500 The Stationery Office 1977 ISBN 0 11 070500 9

16 *Health and Safety (Consultation with Employees) Regulations 1996* SI 1996/1513 The Stationery Office 1996 ISBN 0 11 054839 6

17 Hodgson J T and Darnton A 'The quantative risks of mesothelioma and lung cancer in relation to asbestos exposure' *Annals of Occupational Hygiene* 2000 **44** 565-601

18 *Improved methods for clearance testing and visual assessment of asbestos removal operations* HSL/2001/11 Health and Safety Laboratory 2001

19 ISO/IEC 17025:1999 *General requirements for the competence of testing and calibration laboratories* International Organisation for Standardisation 1999

20 *Application of ISO/IEC 17025 for asbestos sampling and testing* LAB 30 United Kingdom Accreditation Service 2002

21 ISO 17020 International Standard published as BS EN 45004:1995 *General criteria for the operation of various types of bodies performing inspection* British Standards Institution ISBN 0 580 24538 1

22 BS EN ISO/IEC 17024:2003 *Conformity assessment. General requirements for bodies operating certification of persons* British Standards Institution ISBN 0 580 41811 1

23 *A guide to the Asbestos (Licensing) Regulations 1983 as amended. The Asbestos (Licensing) Regulations 1983. Guidance on Regulations* L11 (Second edition) HSE Books 1999 ISBN 0 7176 2435 8

24 *Confined Spaces Regulations 1997* SI 1997/1713 The Stationery Office 1997 ISBN 0 11 064643 6

25 *Respiratory protective equipment at work: A practical guide* HSG53 (Second edition) HSE Books 2004 ISBN 0 7176 2904 X

26 *Fit testing of respiratory protective equipment facepieces* OC 282/28 Operational Circular HSE 2003

27 Directive 2003/18/EC of the 27th March 2003 amending Council Directive 83/477/EEC on the protection of workers from the risks related to exposure to asbestos at work L97 48-52 *Official Journal of the European Union* 15 April 2003

28 *Man-made mineral fibre: Airborne number concentration by phase-contrast light microscopy* MDHS59 HSE Books 1988 ISBN 0 7176 0319 9

29 *Fibres in air: Guidance on the discrimination between fibre types in samples of airborne dust on filters using microscopy* MDHS87 HSE Books 1999 ISBN 0 7176 1487 5

30 Rooker S J et al 'The Visibility of Fibres by Phase Contrast Microscopy' *Journal of American Industrial Hygiene Association* 1982 **43** 505-515

31 Brown P W et al 'Developments in the RICE asbestos fibre counting scheme 1992-2000' *Annals of Occupational Hygiene* 2002 **46** 329-339

32 Walton W H and Beckett S T 'A microscope eyepiece graticule for the evaluation of fibrous dusts' *Annals of Occupational Hygiene* 1977 **20** 19-24

33 BS 7011-2.1:1989 *Consumable accessories for light microscopes. Slides. Specification for dimensions and optical properties* British Standards Institution ISBN 0 580 16816 6; BS 7011-3.1:1989 *Consumable accessories for light microscopes. Cover glasses. Specification for dimensions and optical properties* British Standards Institution ISBN 0 580 16823 9

34 Cherrie J W et al 'The influence of fibre density on the assessment of fibre concentration using the membrane filter method' *Journal of American Industrial Hygiene Association* 1986 **47** (8) 465-474

35   Iles P J and Johnston A M 'Problems of asbestos fibre counting in the presence of fibre -fibre and particle-fibre overlap' *Annals of Occupational Hygiene* 1984 **27** 389-404

36   *The reproducibility of asbestos counts* RR18 HSE Books 1982 ISBN 0 7176 0101 3

37   ISO/IEC 17025:1999 *General requirements for the competence of testing and calibration laboratories* International Organisation for Standardisation 1999

38   *The expression of uncertainty in testing* LAB 12 United Kingdom Accreditation Service 2000

39   *The expression of uncertainty and confidence in measurement* M 3003 United Kingdom Accreditation Service 1997

40   Bradbury S et al *RMS Dictionary of light microscopy: Microscopy handbook* 15 Oxford Science Publishers1989 ISBN 0 19 856421 X

41   Deer W A et al *Rock forming minerals, Volume 3: Sheet silicates* Longmans 1962 ISBN 0 582 46211 8

42   Deer W A et al *Rock forming minerals, Volume 2: Chain silicates* Longmans 1962 ISBN 0 582 46210 X

43   Michaels L, Chissick S S 'Chapter 2 The mineralogy of asbestos' *Asbestos. Properties, applications and hazards Volume 1* John Wiley and Sons Ltd 1979 ISBN 0 471 99698 X

44   Hodgson A A *Fibrous silicates: Lecture Series 1965, Number 4* The Royal Institute of Chemistry 1966 ISBN 0 854 04037 4

45   Michaels L and Chissick S S 'Chapter 3 Chemistry and physics of asbestos' A*sbestos. Properties, applications and hazards Volume 1* John Wiley and Sons Ltd 1979 ISBN 0 471 99698 X

46   Hodgson A A *Scientific advances in asbestos, 1967-85* Anjalena Publications 1986 ISBN 0 95101481 1

47   Walton W H 'The nature, hazards and assessment of occupational exposure to airborne asbestos dust: A review' *Annals of Occupational Hygiene* 1982 **25** (2) 117-247

48   Prentice J and Keech M *Alteration of asbestos with heat: Microscopy and analysis* 1989

49   Laughlin G J and McCrone W C '*The effect of heat on the microscopical properties of asbestos' The Microscope* 1989 **37** 9-15

50   Iles P J and Jeyaratnam M A *A study of heat degraded chrysotile, amosite and crocidolite by X-ray powder diffraction and optical microscopy* (IR/L/DD/89/1) HSE 1989

51   McCrone W C *Asbestos identification* (Second edition) McCrone Research Institute 1987 ISBN 0 904962 11 3

52   *Control of Substances Hazardous to Health Regulations 2002* SI 2002/2677 The Stationery Office 2002 ISBN 0 11 042919 2

53   BS 7258-1:1994 *Laboratory fume cupboards. Specification for safety and performance* British Standards Insitution 1994 ISBN 0 580 22702 2

54   Hughes D *Literature survey and design study of fume cupboards and fume dispersal systems* Science Reviews 1980 ISBN 0 905927 50 8

55   *Bulk asbestos reference minerals for optical microscope identification: Preparation, evaluation and validation* CRR159 HSE Books 1997 ISBN 0 7176 1479 4

56   Hartshorne N H and Stuart A *Chrystals and the polarising microscope* (Fourth edition) Edward Arnold 1970 ISBN 0 71312256 0

57   McCrone W C et al *Polarised light microscopy* McCrone Research Institute 1979 ISBN 0 250 40262 9

58   Dorling M and Zussman J 'Characteristics of asbestiform and non-asbestiform amphiboles' *Lithos* **20** 469-489

59   Davis J M G et al 'Variations in the carcinogenicity of tremolite dust samples of differing morphology' *Annals of the New York Academy of Sciences* 1991 **643** 473-490

60   Kelse J W and Thompson C S 'The regulatory and mineralogical definitions of asbestos and their impact on amphibole dust analysis' *Journal of The American Industrial Hygiene Association* 1989 **50** (11) 613-622

61   Wylie A G *Discriminating amphibole cleavage fragments from asbestos: Rationale and methodology.* Proceedings of the VIIth International Pneumoconiosis Conference (Pittsburgh August 1988), DHHS (NIOSH) Publication 90108 part 2 November 1990 1065-1069

62   *Recommendations for the sampling and identification of asbestos products* Technical Note 3 Asbestos Research Council 1978

63   Monkman L J 'Procedures for the detection and identification of asbestos and other fibres in fibrous inorganic materials' *Annals of Occupational Hygiene* 1979 **22** 127-139

64   Prentice J 'Detection and identification of asbestos' *Annals of Occupational Hygiene* 1980 **23** 311-313

65   Langer A M et al 'Distinguishing between amphibole asbestos fibres and elongate cleavage fragments of their non-asbestos analogues' *Mechanisms in fibre carcinogenesis* 1991 253-267 ISBN 0 30 644091 1

66   Churchyard M P and Copeland G K E 'Is it really chrysotile?' *Annals of Occupational Hygiene* 1988 **32** 545-547

67   *Analytical quality in workplace air monitoring* MDHS71 HSE Books 1991 ISBN 0 7176 1263 5

68   *Colour vision* Medical Guidance Note MS7 (Second edition) HSE Books 1987 ISBN 0 11 883950 0

69   *The Carriage of Dangerous Goods and Use of Transportable Pressure Receptacles Regulations 2004* SI 2004/568 The Stationery Office 2004 ISBN 0 11 049063 0

70   *The Environmental Protection Act 1990* The Stationery Office 1990 ISBN 0 10544390 5

71   *The Special Waste Regulations 1996* SI 1996/972 The Stationery Office 1996 ISBN 0 11 054565 6

Further information

HSE priced and free publications are available by mail order from HSE Books,
PO Box 1999, Sudbury, Suffolk CO10 2WA Tel: 01787 881165 Fax: 01787 313995
Website: www.hsebooks.co.uk (HSE priced publications are also available from bookshops
and free leaflets can be downloaded from HSE's website: www.hse.gov.uk.)

For information about health and safety ring HSE's Infoline Tel: 08701 545500
Fax: 02920 859260 e-mail: hseinformationservices@natbrit.com or write to HSE Information
Services, Caerphilly Business Park, Caerphilly CF83 3GG.

The Stationery Office (formerly HMSO) publications are available from PO Box 29,
Norwich NR3 1GN Tel: 0870 600 5522 Fax: 0870 600 5533
e-mail:customer.services@tso.co.uk
Website: www.tso.co.uk (They are also available from bookshops.)

British Occupational Hygiene Society (BOHS)
Suite 2, Georgian House
Great Northern Road
Derby DE1 1LT
Tel: 01332 298101/298087
Fax: 01332 298099
Website: www.bohs.org

Committee for Fibre Measurement (CFM)
Health and Safety Laboratory
Harpur Hill
Buxton
Derbyshire SK17 9JN
Tel: 0114 289 2000
Website: www.hsl.gov.uk

United Kingdom Accreditation Service (UKAS)
21-47 High Street,
Feltham,
Middlesex TW13 4UN
Tel: 0208 917 8400
Website: www.ukas.com

A list of accredited laboratories is available from www.ukas.org

Environment Agency Website: www.environment-agency.gov.uk

Scottish Environment Protection Agency Website: www.sepa.org.uk

Acknowledgement

HSE wishes to acknowledge the assistance given by Working Group Two of the Committee
on Fibre Measurement in the production of Appendices 1 and 2. CFM/WG2 consisted of
Mr J Addison (John Addison Consultancy), Mrs T Boyle (HSE), Dr G Burdett (HSL),
Mr L Davies (Institute of Occupational Medicine), Ms J Prentice (McCrone Scientific Ltd),
Mr W Sanderson (Casella Environmental Ltd), Mr D McAuliffe (UKAS) and Mr B E Tylee (HSL).

Glossary of acronyms

ACM	Asbestos-containing material
ACOP	Approved Code of Practice
AIB	Asbestos insulating board
APF	Assigned protection factor
ASLIC	The Asbestos (Licensing) Regulations 1983
BOHS	British Occupational Hygiene Society
CAWR	Control of Asbestos at Work Regulations 2002
CFM	Committee on fibre measurement
FF(P3)	Filtering facepiece (respirator)
HEPA	High efficiency particulate arrestor
HSC	Health and Safety Commission
HSE	Health and Safety Executive
HSL	Health and Safety Laboratory
PCM	Phase contrast microscopy
PLM	Polarised light microscopy
PPE	Personal protective equipment
PVA	Polyvinyl acetate
QA	Quality assurance
QC	Quality control
RI	Refractive index
RICE	Regular interlaboratory counting exchange
RPE	Respiratory protective equipment
SLH	Supervisory licence holder
UKAS	United Kingdom Accreditation Service

Printed and published by the Health and Safety Executive   01/05   C50